AVOID

BUILDING

A LIFE

YOU HATE

Bret, this is incomplete without you.

Olivia, your creative brushstrokes
tied the bow. It's going to be fun to
watch how far your gifts take you.

"STORIES ARE EQUIPMENT FOR LIVING."

KENNETH BURKE

TABLE OF CONTENTS

INTRO:

We are afraid. We're afraid we messed up too much or that we are going to mess up. What if we could learn the essentials for building a life we love? We could focus on what matters.

You can learn the 7 mistakes that will build a life you hate. The pages ahead are like overhearing a SightShift coaching conversation. The narration is from the perspective of The Rider. Here's to building a life you love.

# CORE

I sat in the eye of the storm.

Waves crashing against my kayak, cold water spilled onto my clothes and supplies.

All around me lightning struck.

Rain poured incessantly. Another flash of lightning and I saw it. At the four mile mark the river ran close to the highway. Paddling with a ferocity I knew would eventually wear me down, I maneuvered into a yard. The kayak bumped into a rusty car and a loose piece of metal dug itself into the plastic hull.

The dugout was beyond rescuing.

I made my way to the edge of the highway.

A few cars passed; most drivers too focused on the challenging road conditions to notice my presence.

I didn't blame them.

Two more cars approached me.
I stepped an inch closer to the road.

Thumb up. The first one passed by.

The second, a '67 red Ford, pulled over on the shoulder.

DRIVER:
Where are you going?

RIDER:
I need to get back to my car. It's at the 70 West bridge.

DRIVER:
Hop in. I can get you there.

RIDER:
I can't thank you enough. The storm came sooner than I expected.

> The driver slid up the radio's volume nob. We continued on in silence.

RIDER:
Where are you headed?

DRIVER:
Away.

RIDER:
Away from what?

> He peered over at me as if I had strayed from an agreed upon script.

DRIVER:
Away from a stale life. I'm heading West.

RIDER:
What's West?

> He pursed his lips.

DRIVER:
Do you always ask so many questions?

RIDER:
Sorry, it's a habit. I tend to jump right in.

A stretch of silence covered the space between us.

DRIVER:
Well I guess you could say I want a fresh start. A new adventure. Something to get excited about.

RIDER:
Sometimes I dream about running away to Colorado and opening a ski shop. Haven't gone through with it though.

He cleared his throat.

DRIVER:
What holds you back?

RIDER:
A secure identity. One that's not defined by the wins and losses of life.

DRIVER:
A what?

RIDER:
Let me ask you a question. Why are you moving west?

He let out a sigh.

DRIVER:
Great, another question.

RIDER:
Bear with me.

DRIVER:
A fresh start.

RIDER:
Yeah, that's what you said. But why are you really running? What are you hoping will be different out West?

A glint of skepticism flickered through his eyes.

DRIVER:
Yeah, I don't really want to talk about this… it's kind of personal

An orange sign with lights flashing on either side read: Road construction ahead. Be prepared to stop.

His eyes fell to the clock.
Hesitantly, he began.

DRIVER:
I guess I hope I can stop living like everyone else wants me to live. I feel like everyday I have to live up to the pressure of someone else. I know I've made made mistakes along the way, but does that mean I have to spend the rest of my life trying to make up for them?

RIDER:
Do you workout?

DRIVER:
Huh?

RIDER:
Exercise. Do you run or lift weights? Play a sport of some kind?

> The driver pursed his lips, sat up straight in his seat and gripped the steering wheel with both hands.

DRIVER:
Look, I know I have a beer belly going but I don't need your judgment. I have my wife for that.

RIDER:
That's not where I was taking that question.

> He loosened his grip on the steering wheel.

DRIVER:
Yeah, I played some basketball in my day. What does that have to do with anything?

RIDER:
The key to strength training is a stable core. If you excessively focus on building up muscles that are not akin to your core, you set yourself up for injury. You may look like the strongest guy in the gym but your functional health is weak. First you have to build the core muscles to strengthen the joints for a foundation to build upon.

DRIVER:
That makes sense. It sounds like building a home.

RIDER:

Exactly! Without a strong foundation the whole house is set up to crumble. If the foundation is strong the house can endure some structural damage. The same is true for how we build our lives. If we don't start with a secure core a few bad decisions could erode everything.

The driver let out a chuckle.

DRIVER:

Well, it sounds like you have things figured out.

RIDER:

I once thought I did. In my 20s I had success that surpassed any and all of my expectations. My wife and I built our first house and walked in with over 25% equity. I started giving to a retirement fund at age 21. For a short time, I became a paper millionaire through an investment. But the truth of it is, I didn't understand who I was. I chased performance. I squandered everything through some bad decisions. By the start of my 30s I was sitting on my front porch with an eviction notice on the door.

A long pause.

DRIVER:

Did you think about it? I mean, leaving everything behind and moving to Colorado?

RIDER:

I thought about it. When you don't know how you are going to feed or shelter your wife and three daughters, you ask yourself some tough questions.

DRIVER:

Like what?

RIDER:

Like, "Who are you?"

> He tapped his fingers against the steering wheel.
> A familiar silence filled the car.

DRIVER:

Some days I ask myself why I'm doing this. Why do I keep going? Wouldn't it be easier to just run away?

RIDER:

Those same questions raced through my mind when I found that eviction note. In that moment I realized the central issue. Problems made me feel bad about who I was. I had built who I was around how well I matched up to my standard of performance. No matter how far I ran I would always have to answer, "Who are you?" If I didn't come up with a sound answer for that, apart from what I accomplished in work or who I was in relationship with, then every negative thing that happened would answer the question for me.

DRIVER:

So, how did you answer it?

RIDER:

I realized that all problems could lead to this place of exploring who you are apart from what you do, no matter how big or how small. Rather than diminishing who you are, you can use your problems to get creative and grow into a bigger capacity for life. Once you learn how to utilize your problems, you develop deeper resiliency and a greater appreciation for your skillset.

For most people, problems shut them down. They lock up and allow their issues to suffocate them. In response, they rigidly try to force life to bend around what they want. If it doesn't work out to their specifications, they throw a fit or give up.

> The driver shook his head irritably.
> His patience was fading.

DRIVER:
I've heard this before. They tell me I should be thankful for all my problems. But I've been through some shit that I wouldn't wish on my worst enemy. Are you telling me when you were sitting on your porch with an eviction notice on the door, you were glad that happened?

RIDER:
There wasn't an ounce of my being that felt good about what was happening. I fell asleep that night not knowing where we would sleep the next night. It was awful. And I hoped my kids would never have to experience the sense of failure I felt in that moment. I'm not saying you have to be thankful for all of your problems. And I don't hope that bad times will enter anyone's life. But I do hope that when bad times come, because they will, that you can find the gift of knowing you are not defined by what is happening in that moment.

> I motioned out the window.
> He kept his focus in front of him.

Think about this road we're driving down right now. There

is a ditch on each side of the road. In the left ditch there are people that falsely believe they should be thankful that bad things are happening in their lives. The people in this ditch are lying to themselves. They're masquerading an attitude they don't truly believe and trying to fake their way through the season.

The people in the right ditch associate themselves with their problems. Those people are defined by their circumstances and mistakes.

The key idea for understanding these ditches is the difference between shame and guilt. Shame is when you feel bad about who you are. Guilt is when you feel bad about what you have done. Those in the left ditch won't acknowledge reality because the shame is too painful. Those in the right ditch believe a shame-based lie about who they are because of the circumstances they are in.

When you accept this lie as a truth, you start to believe a lie about your identity. You start to believe you are not enough.

If you don't learn who you are apart from your problems, you are going to push through those low moments in a panicked state of activity that will turn people away. When you separate who you are, you can calm down, build a long-term vision and tackle the most urgent and influential tasks first.

The key is learning to put a sequence of pauses in your thinking before it spins out of control. If you're stuck in one of the two ditches your response to the problems dehumanizes you.

DRIVER:
How?

RIDER:
In the left ditch you willfully strive through the moment
in a superficial way. You push people away because no one
wants to be connected to that except others who are going
through the exact same motions, providing the same life-
hindering results.

In the right ditch you become a less human form
of yourself because you believe these problems and
circumstances sum up who you are. The right problems
mix and you start to believe you are less than, that you don't
belong, that you are not enough.

> He shifted his gaze out the window.
> The ditches passing across his eyes,
> like a projection he could no longer hide.

DRIVER:
I feel like that sometimes. No matter how many times
I try to tell myself that I'm enough, there's a thousand
other voices in my head telling me I'm not. Maybe it's fear.
Maybe's it's the truth.

RIDER:
The universe has a way of designing a customized path for
each of us that brings fear so close it feels like it's breathing
down our necks. It drives us to our knees and we are left
with only two choices, or rather two ditches. We either
hype our way through it by proving ourselves or we
succumb to the pressure and give up a little bit of who we
are by hiding. When we take either of these extremes we
become a worse version of ourselves. Life dehumanizes us.

The decision I made on that porch was to stop running away, to stop numbing out, and to re-humanize where life dehumanized me.

He pressed a coffee cup to his lips and chuckled.

DRIVER:
Wow. I didn't realize that picking you up meant picking up a counseling session.

RIDER:
I'm sorry. I guess being out there on the river has a way of reconnecting me to stuff I'm passionate about.

Another long pause ensued.
He shook his head softly.

DRIVER:
Don't apologize for that. You have my attention.

He sighed, running a hand over his face.

I'm just so deep into life right now; it's hard to imagine anything changing. My kids are almost teenagers and I have spent decades building what everyone sees as a successful career.

RIDER:
It sounds to me like you're on the right path.

DRIVER:
By running away?

RIDER:
By getting in touch with your deepest desires.

It all starts with living authentically. No proving. No hiding. Not trying to accomplish something to make you feel whole or complete.

Be who you are.

Out of that secure being, approach life. Build your life around the passion of authentic desire. Pour that into what you do. Over time that passion will attract people around you. Then you'll build the party you want to join rather than try to break into someone else's party. Find your path. Pursue your Mission. Build your party.

We have the tendency to mix the order up. We go after an achievement to make ourselves feel whole, or use up all our energy to fit into a certain relationship we believe will complete us. But all of that is an inauthentic expression of who we are. When problems arise, anxiety sets in and cripples us from approaching life from an offensive position. Instead, we react defensively.

The sequence is: Be who you are. Out of that comes authentic doing. Then you have the relationships you desire.

DRIVER:
You talk about getting in touch with your deepest desires, but sometimes my strongest desire is to just sit on the couch and play video games. Or worse, my desires feel scary and I don't want to admit them. That doesn't seem very noble or productive.

RIDER:
I would say it's a question of motives.
There was a season of life when I was hustling to just make

it day-to-day. There were nights when I was getting home with nothing to show for the day's work. The anxiety of not knowing how we were going to get groceries the next day ruined any chance I had at sleeping. During those late nights I was awake until 3 a.m. trying to calm my heart rate down. Trying to think of a way out of that season and into the next one.

One particular night, with only $2.57 in the bank account, I bought a zombie show off the Internet for $1.99. A thousand sound financial principles could explain why that was a bad decision. However, for me it was the difference between having $2.57 or 58 cents. More importantly, it was the difference between lying awake anxious or calming my anxieties and being ushered into dreamland.

An incredulous smirk escaped his lips.

DRIVER:
Zombie's calmed your heart rate?

RIDER:
It sounds counterproductive, but I needed a story to consume me. It's all about creating optimal internal conditions. There is not much in life we can control other than our internal world. Our responses to the uncontrollable external circumstances are dictated by our internal condition. We can't build perfect external conditions to create the path or responses we desire. The focus changes to creating optimal internal conditions to meet the demands of whatever external circumstances arise.

For me, in that moment, $1.99 was not a wasteful binge of escape. It was an investment in my internal condition during a season of intense hustling so I could wake up the next day refreshed and ready to tackle it again. The key to getting me out of that hole was unblocking the creative expression of who I am to solve the problems of life.

I could have committed the bulk of my energy to the "ditch of hype" that would keep me chasing fantasies or the "ditch of being a victim" that would keep me defeated. Instead, I began living from a secure core and using those problems to grow.

DRIVER:
It sounds like you do a lot of investment in yourself. It seems to be a little too self-centered for my comfort.

RIDER:
Have you ever flown in a commercial airplane?

DRIVER:
Yes, plenty of times.

RIDER:
Then you know during the safety announcements before takeoff, the flight attendant always instructs you to secure your air mask first before helping others. Apply that to your life. All you're doing is making sure you are healthy before projecting your responses and passions onto the situation. If you walk into staff meetings depleted, wishing for a different job, you won't be able to lead in an authentic way.

DRIVER:
That makes sense. I guess if I was down to $2.57 in the bank account and was going to buy a movie I would pick one my daughters enjoyed so we could all watch it together.

RIDER:

Motives make the difference. Even the noblest acts can cause you to become a worse version of yourself. I've known of people who run homeless shelters frustrated with "Good Samaritans" who randomly feed the homeless. For the Good Samaritan, doing good for less fortunate makes them feel amazing. But are they doing it to give something to the homeless or get something from their charitable activity? What's the motive? Those managing the shelters are frustrated because now the homeless don't use the resources of the shelter for a more holistic care and recovery.

To say it another way, I could buy a movie to watch with my daughters and invite them to spend the evening together with me. Afterward if one of them said she didn't enjoy the movie and my response is, "Aren't you thankful I hung out with you?" She would look at me like I'm crazy. In that situation, I arranged the family activity to get something from them rather than give something to them. I did it to feel good about myself.

When we live out of our insecurities we approach what we do, needing the achievement or the relationship to make us feel whole. We will be blocked up from bringing our authentic self to the moment.

DRIVER:

So how do you figure out what these insecurities are?

RIDER:

That's a great question. My answer is going to sound crazy but bear with me.

You uncover the insecurity by imagining the worst possible scenario.

Making a quick lane change, he glanced over at me.

DRIVER:
You were right about the crazy part. That sounds like a miserable way to make it through tough times. You're basically setting your course for disaster.

RIDER:
Don't get me wrong. I am a believer in the power of imagining a positive future. But you have to be careful because you might use that to chase a fantasy and distract yourself from present pain.

You can actually avoid some pain by imagining the worst possible scenario because your response in that scenario reveals the fear that is driving you.

It's like lifting weights. If you squat with no weight, your form will be functionally sound. Adding weight to a barbell on your shoulders increases the stress. Add enough weight and your body starts to compensate in weak points by distorting your form. If you keep lifting this way, your workouts will do more harm than good in the long run. Imagining the negative scenario is like adding weight to the barbell. It will reveal the weak points in your position.

As I was sitting on that porch with an eviction notice on the door, it didn't take much imagining for me. I was a day away from selling everything I owned and taking my wife and kids to the streets. Picking up another leadership book wasn't going to help me in that situation. I couldn't rebuild off hype. At that point, I was scraping bottom.

Being faced with the worst-case scenario I remember imagining what it would be like to look at myself in the mirror if that happened. What would I say to myself?

"Look what happened because of your screw up. You suck as a father and as a husband. You are not worthy of this family."

Or I could look in the mirror and say, "This circumstance does not diminish who I am."

In that moment I realized that I was being weighed down by my doubt in feeling that I wasn't worthy because of my performance. Those feelings of doubt put a wedge between between the people I love and their inability to make me feel worthy enough. It was blocking me from bringing my creative self to solve the problem.

The problem presented a clear picture. I was building who I was around what I did and what others thought of me. It taught me that I have an identity that is not defined by the achievements and relationships in my life.

> The driver leaned back in his seat and clicked on cruise control.
>
> The air conditioner blew out air, ruffling pages of the map beside me.
>
> He sighed, his words coming out in a mutter.

DRIVER:
That is a lot to chew on.

RIDER:

It's freedom. It's available to everyone if you take the time to get underneath your motivations and uncover the fear.

I think of a business executive who doesn't accomplish his goal at work. His boss is angry with his performance and he doesn't get the bonus he anticipated. If he keeps playing out the scenario, what happens if he doesn't get the bonus? Maybe he can't deliver on a promise he made to his family. So he looks at himself in the mirror and imagines a conversation with his wife where he tells her he didn't get the bonus.

"Honey, I didn't get the bonus. Therefore, I am..."

However he fills in the blank reveals what he falsely believes about who he is.

"I didn't get the bonus. Therefore, I am not worthy."

"Therefore, I am not safe."

"Therefore, I am not going to be cared for."

The ambitious doctor who excelled through years of schooling finally gets hired at a prestigious hospital in town. What drove her to pursue that particular hospital? The ambition itself is not dangerous but the motive could be. If it was to please someone else, there is a midlife crisis in her future. She could become an expert at burying the stress symptoms but eventually they come out. When that happens, a new husband with a convertible won't fix her problems.

The athlete, who believes that not winning inherently

means inadequacy, believes he is defined by his performance. He is going to be so attached to the result, the pressure will extract the joy of being in the moment and he will get the result he was afraid to get.

Every successful startup entrepreneur has a library of stories about failures along the way. Even if it succeeds, building who you are around that success is just as dangerous. In result, you become a worse version of yourself. If you don't learn to use your problems and failures to promote growth within yourself, they will end your business before it ever starts. It's best to face it before you ever reach the boiling point of that insecure identity.

DRIVER:
That sounds like some intense introspection. I'm not really the imagining and introspective type.

RIDER:
Introspection is like a muscle. For most people it has atrophied because of a lack of use. I used to play a lot of basketball. I was a strong right-handed player but I couldn't play well with my left hand. So every time I drove to the basket I would drive right and jump off my left foot for a layup. My friends tell me this is ridiculous, but I believe after several years of only shooting right-handed layups my left leg became stronger than my right.

If we look at our internal core through a similar lens, we will recognize how our behavior is compensating for these insecurities in our identity. Most people don't invest that kind of attention into themselves. Instead they move through life positioning and posturing to get others to meet the needs of their identity. They are navigating life blind to these issues and suffer unnecessary pain through self-sabotaging choices.

DRIVER:
This makes me wonder how many mistakes I've made over the last 10 years that I'm not even aware of.

RIDER:
From my experience, there are seven mistakes everyone makes but few learn from. I'd be happy to share the other six with you but I could use a pit stop first.

DRIVER:
I'd make a stop for you but the closest rest stop is another 30 miles down the road. Can you make it that long?

RIDER:
It's OK. I'm already soaking wet. Pull over here. I'll run under that tree canopy to get some covering.

DRIVER:
Whatever you say, man. Good luck.

The car came to a stop, yet we had just begun.

# FEAR

The wheels of our car sped through
burnished puddles of rainwater.

Still a sheet of rain loomed in the distance.

We had settled into a rhythm of conversation;
one that skipped beats and rests,
one that was not bound but restless.

DRIVER:
What a terrible day. You may have picked the worst day
possible to go out on the river.

RIDER:
I wouldn't say that. I was going to get wet anyway and the
storm created some wicked rapids. The challenge was fun.

The driver just shook his head.

DRIVER:
I see what you're doing. Thankful for all your problems?

RIDER:
You were listening.

DRIVER:
I'm hearing what you're saying, but, I don't know…

His voice trailed off.

I don't think I've completely grasped it yet. But keep going, I'm still listening.

RIDER:
During that season of deep struggle when I was hustling to make it day-to-day I learned how to be happy regardless of my circumstances.

DRIVER:
I have a hard time imagining anyone circling around a fire pit singing Kumbaya in the midst of utter personal and financial turmoil.

RIDER:
Remember the ditches? We aren't hyping ourselves into a false reality where problems don't exist. It's learning that we are not defined by our circumstances. When you reach that point you become free of the fear that drives you.

DRIVER:
What do you mean by "free of the fear"?

RIDER:
Do you know anyone who always has something to prove? They have to outdo you in every conversation to show how much worse they have it or how better they are.

DRIVER:
Definitely. We call him "One Up". Everything you say he has to one up you. My kid hits his first home run, but his kid hits a grand slam to win the game. I get a bonus at work, but he gets promoted to director.

RIDER:
That's the perfect nickname! When I get home and tell the story about this trip, I have a friend who will probably counter with a story about surviving a plane crash and

being stranded on a deserted island.

RIDER:
Some of their stories are entertaining and worth contributing to the exchange. Most of the time, though, these people are struggling with celebrating who you are and what's happening in your life. They have to find a way to bring it back to them so they can prove they are superior.

DRIVER:
I know what you're talking about. It's like they're radiating pride. It's hard for me to even want to be around people like that.

RIDER:
That's the thing; they push people away. On the surface it seems prideful but I've learned it's not a bloated sense of self. It's insecurity. It's fear. They feel insecure about who they are so they're trying to prove something to others.

Most likely you also know people who are very withdrawn. They are afraid to bring the full weight of who they are to a situation. They're hiding. They are on the opposite end of the spectrum of insecurity.

These are the extremes, but there is proving and hiding happening in everyday circumstances for each of us. Think back to the last conflict you had with someone you are in relationship with, maybe a loved one or a co-worker. Our insecurities don't allow us to modulate that tension in a healthy way. We become rigid, digging in our heels and building up walls to protect ourselves from the threat we feel to our identity. We hide within ourselves first and then we give up or we prove and exert pressure to manipulate the situation in our favor. We use words like "always" and "never" to win the argument.

Underneath the conflict, someone felt insecure and threatened, and that triggered another insecure reaction, which resulted in escalating conflict.

No one is immune to this fear. The key is becoming aware of the fear that is driving our insecure identity.

He glanced down at his wedding band,
rubbing it between his thumb and pinky finger.

DRIVER:
Last week my wife and I had a huge argument. She wanted to go on a trip with her friends. I got angry. We haven't been on a trip together in two years. I don't know why I was so angry but it really pissed me off.

> Replaying it in his mind,
> he sighed, shaking his head softly.

I said some really hurtful things to her. An hour later we were fighting about money, her nosy parents, and why I don't take out the trash. It was probably this fear you're talking about, right?

RIDER:
Absolutely. Once you get to this level of understanding, you begin to see things that are others are ignoring. Most people are just dealing with the surface-level issue that is right in front of them but they are missing the deeper reality. It's why the same problems seem to always resurface. We focus on the symptom and never address the root of the issue. There are bigger clues we need to see.

When I notice the times I power up to prove something or feel the need to hide out of fear, I take that as a signal that something else is happening underneath the surface. I feel insecure about who I am, so I deconstruct that moment to uncover the fear that is driving me.

In your example the fear was probably related to where

you fit into your wife's priorities. You were probably asking yourself, "Why doesn't she want to take a trip with me?"

> There was a brief silence.
> He looked down at his ring;
> his restless fingers easing into a stillness.
> I continued on.

We've talked some about intimate relationships. This also applies to our work environments. When you gain precise awareness of your fear then you can understand the source of your insecurity.

DRIVER:
I'm not sure I want to have a precise awareness of my fear. How do I get to a place where I can actively acknowledge something like that?

RIDER:
It's a daunting idea. Some people are afraid that if they are not needed they'll feel lost. They don't invest in others or develop and empower leaders around them. Instead, they develop systems that keep them as the essential hub. They set it up so the company can't survive without them.

There is another fear that causes leaders to become like Chicken Little. They are in a position of authority as the leader but they don't inspire confidence. They don't stare down the opposing forces. Instead, they amplify what could go wrong. Rather than inspiring through hope they bolt with fear, testing the commitment of followers.

The other reaction is to kick the can further down the road; gloss over reality and ignore the glaring problems. People who have this reaction postpone decisions, afraid to address critical issues. Their company's quarterly reports have thousands of footnotes trying to prove and hide. They are afraid people will abandon them unless everything is smooth, so they construct a false peace.

For some, the fear is that they can't do it. If you fear that you don't have what it takes you will either jump in blindly, throwing strategy out the window, or you'll be disengaged and withdrawn. You respond this way because you don't want to feel the vulnerability of assessing strengths and weaknesses and how to develop new skills. You probably excel in one area but feel foolish in others.

For some people fear makes them feel like they have to win big to be worth a lot. These people are always building a future fantasy rather than addressing present concerns. The problem with this is that they are burning others out to get there and eventually they will burn out too.

There are other people who are afraid of who they are so they talk a big game but don't deliver. Hype is coursing through their veins to the point it's confused with motivation. They get hooked on adrenaline. For a moment they will feel relieved that they haven't been labeled the fraud they believe they are. Rather than learning they are not a fraud and finding intrinsic motivation, the external hype just fades.

Fear drives some of us to miss the present and obsess on the past. When we don't know who we are, not only do we find ourselves caught up in the moment and lose sight of what is happening but we also build a shrine to the past. Anxiety of the present and the nail-biting unknown of the future causes us to stay stuck in nostalgia. We are afraid the ground beneath us is going to give way so we look for whatever sure footing we can find.

DRIVER:
You know, sometimes it's easier; pushing people away, putting up walls. Sometimes I think fear protects us from the things that will hurt us the most.

RIDER:

It's scary, isn't it? Letting others get close? And maybe it seems easier that way, but all of those walls we build up, amount to nothing genuine in our lives. I knew this guy in high school. His name was Sam. He told amazing stories and made people laugh, but at the end of the day he couldn't draw people into his leadership. He was fake and everyone knew it except for him. His walls were rigid and imposing. People would try to get close to him, but he'd always end up pushing them away, afraid to be vulnerable.

> The driver clicked on cruise control and sunk down in his seat. Staring off into the long strip of interstate in front of us, he shook his head.

DRIVER:

Man, that sounds miserable.

RIDER:

I think Sam would have agreed with you.

DRIVER:

Is it strange that I see this fear in multiple aspects of my life? Or am I just really problematic?

RIDER:

It's not strange. Some people resent being passed over for a promotion or believe they should get that big win but they won't put themselves out there in the big pond. Fear has kept them from tapping into their uniqueness and bringing their voice to the table.

The key to uncovering this is getting to a place where your fear comes to the surface.

> He clicked off cruise control and sat up in his seat. A few cars passed us, but he maintained his speed.

DRIVER:
Those are totally resonating. I can see how that argument with my wife wasn't just about her trip with her friends. And I see the reaction to our new initiative at work in a different light. There was way more to it. Now I'm wondering what else I've done out of fear.

RIDER:
Well, not to be too discouraging, but there's probably a lot.

It's like looking into a mirror. It can be hard to see reality because our brains want a narrative that shames us or blames others. When we get a glimpse of reality our natural instinct is to blame someone or something so we don't have to feel the weight of our fear. Or we shame ourselves into believing we deserve bad things that happen.

These fears unconsciously drive all the choices we make. Think about why you bought this truck you're driving. You probably made a list of pros and cons to help you make the best decision. What you didn't realize is that fear was shaping your perception of what was 'pro' and what was 'con'.

Think of the last time you reacted blindly out of rage or were manipulative through passive anger. The internal driver was fear.

DRIVER:
I have a ton of those examples. I can see how it pops up for me all over the place, but I don't know how to change it. How do you control the fear when it is happening subconsciously?

RIDER:
Many self-help books or speakers will hype you into believing you can just choose a different reality. They'll say, "Choose to be happy today." Or they force an external habit onto your life in hopes that it will transform the internal. It

doesn't work that way.

Consider a scenario where my daughter tells me she doesn't believe I love her. To help her, I write on a note card, "Daddy loves you," and I instruct her to read it 100 times every day. My wife sees her walking around the house with furrowed eyebrows reading the card over and over: "Daddy loves you. Daddy loves you. Daddy loves you."

How long will she have to do that until she truly believes I love her?

DRIVER:
That sounds ridiculous.

RIDER:
Exactly! That is how most of us try to conquer the fears we believe about ourselves. We fixate on an external, hoping it will make it to our internal. It sounds good when motivational speakers shout it from a stage, and it can be effective in the short-term, but eventually it wears off. You get tired and worn down and you revert back to your default setting. To avoid the trap, you have to create a new internal reality, a new baseline.

The other response to my daughter telling me she doesn't believe I love her is to pick her up and hug her and whisper it into her ear; to take her to the pool for the day and play with her all weekend; to help her with her homework when she is stuck on a problem.

With this response it shifts away from superficial self-help, and develops into deep internal change. I am helping her see, feel, and hear a different reality about who she is. I'm helping her receive truth. She is loved. She is celebrated. She belongs. Her needs are not a problem.

DRIVER:

What I hear you saying is an experience is more powerful than knowledge?

RIDER:

So powerful that it actually rewires the brain. So many people think we are who we are and we aren't changing. But modern neuroscience has proven otherwise. The ability our brains possess to change is called neuroplasticity. We are constantly changing based on our experiences – if we position ourselves to let those new experiences in. This really becomes powerful when we develop the ability to create new experiences to counteract the fear we feel.

You won't become invincible to the point where you'll never hurt again. Pain is a part of life. You will be hurt again. You will feel lonely again. You will feel inadequate again. But with this level of awareness you can learn to keep going, happy with who you are regardless of the circumstances.

DRIVER:

This is heavy stuff. I guess it kind of overwhelms me. I've spent over 10 years building a successful career, sustaining a marriage and raising kids. We have our patterns and routines and a template that works.

I smirked as we came to stop behind a line of cars.

RIDER:

Works so well you're sitting here with me...

DRIVER:

Good point. I'm just saying it seems like an intimidating task to turn it all around overnight. Wouldn't it be easier to just start over elsewhere?

RIDER:

You're right. It won't turn around overnight. A lot of habits and patterns have built up callouses over time so you no longer feel the pain. That will take time to deconstruct and rebuild. But it's a better option than running away because the same issues are going to resurface unless you deal with the root cause. And judging by that picture on your dashboard, you have a beautiful family; one worth investing in the process of transformation.

> His eyes fell from the road to the picture;
> a collage of smiling faces.
> A reminder of all the reasons not to run.

DRIVER:
They are pretty great.

RIDER:
The best place to start is to find one small moment where you felt yourself "prove" or "hide" and call it out. When you bring it into the light it can't continue to grow in the darkness below the surface.

We recently found mold in the basement of our new house. The previous owners tried to spray paint over it and encapsulate it rather than correctly treat it. Their remedy covered it up for the short-term but it eventually grew out of the encapsulation. When we moved in we had to do a thorough treatment by airing out the basement after spraying a compound to kill the mold.

Our internal world works the same way. We can't just cover up the moldy parts and hope they go away. We have to open the windows, air it out, and shine light onto the things we are afraid to admit about ourselves.

If you can bring just one small moment of proving or hiding to your conscious mind, your brain will get excited about the recognition and start to organize around the awareness. This initiates the trajectory of change.

We changed lanes in an attempt to beat the traffic. The driver flicked a piece of dust off the picture of his family.

DRIVER:
What was your one small moment?

I sat back in my seat, a familiar memory casing my mind.

RIDER:
It all started when one of my friends told me I had issues with feeling worthy. At first I wasn't exactly sure what he meant. A few weeks later I took my daughter out to lunch on her birthday and as we sat in that restaurant I found myself asking her a series of questions about how much she enjoyed our lunch date. "Are you having fun with Daddy? Aren't you glad I took you out to lunch on your birthday?" I heard myself asking those questions and I realized that underneath them was a need to feel worthy as a parent. It was my first small moment, but a massive moment of awareness. My friend had shed light on my internal mold.

DRIVER:
As you tell that story I'm thinking about how my wife complains about my driving.

I tightened my seatbelt, peering up at the rear view mirror.

RIDER:
I wasn't going to say anything because I'm thankful for the ride, but for the past 30 minutes I've never been more thankful for a seat belt.

DRIVER:
Oh no, you too?

RIDER:
Like I said, I'm thankful for the ride.

DRIVER:
That's right. I'm all you got!

>   We shared a chuckle over my helplessness.

As I process what you're saying I'm wondering if my impatience in driving is showing up in other areas of my life.

RIDER:
It probably is.

DRIVER:
I feel like I project my anxiousness onto my kids.

RIDER:
You are on the verge of opening up your awareness and developing eyes that see.

DRIVER:
They would probably appreciate me figuring out why I'm so impatient.

RIDER:
No one wishes you would be less patient with them.

DRIVER:
And my wife would appreciate me getting fewer speeding tickets.

RIDER:
This is the catalyst of life change.

When fear is in control, everything is perceived as a false

threat to our identity – even in the smallest of moments.

DRIVER:
What do you mean by "false" threat?

RIDER:
Remember we talked earlier about our identity being secure and stable? It's a false threat because no one can take from who we are. No human being is responsible for our worth, our dignity, our safety, our feeling of love. It is not sustainable to expect another human being to meet those needs with perfect abundance. It will only foster a toxic relationship. Even if they could meet those needs for a while, it's still an external gift. What we really need is internal.

We need to be in a place where internally we believe who we are in truth and we're not succumbing to the fear. Then when we interact in relationships that meet those desires we can enjoy them and be thankful for them without needing them in order to feel complete.

The goal is to gain clarity on how we compensate for the stress and pressures of life. Think back to the example of squatting with weights on the bar.

We want to draw attention to those weak points. If you don't become aware of those you will keep adding to the barbell and the load will get heavier. Your body will distort its form, compensating for the weak foundation. Next thing you know you're in a relationship for 10 years, bouncing off each other's fears without really knowing who you are; or you're 15 years into a career where you still haven't learned how to bring the unobstructed expression of who you are to what you do.

Is that making sense?

DRIVER:
I think so. I used to workout with a personal trainer and he would drive me crazy with how meticulous he was with proper form. All I wanted to do was get stronger, faster and he kept taking weight off the rack.

DRIVER:
But, I'm not sure I completely understand this idea of bringing the unobstructed expression of who you are to what you do.

RIDER:
The simplest way for me to explain it is this:

You can have certainty in who you are. You will never have certainty in what you're going to do – in your case, it's your career. It's the thing you're attempting, the goal you're going after. There is no certainty you will get the result you want.

The best you can do is have certainty in who you are. With that certainty you will have clarity in what you are to do. You will have a focus that ignites your passion. You will bring the unobstructed expression of who you are because you're not doing it for someone else.

Then you'll have confidence in your relationships because you're not expecting someone else to make you feel whole.

So if we ask ourselves, "What is going to block confidence in relationships and clarity in what we do?" The answer is not being certain in who we are.

How do we know where we are uncertain in who we are? Pay attention to the fear.

DRIVER:
That seems pretty straightforward.

RIDER:
The subtle, simple solutions are always the best.

He pondered that as we drove on.

In the distance, there was an empty park with a cluster of trees surrounding it.

Beside it was a steep hill. The grass was sparkling with remnants from the afternoon's showers.

Hey, it looks like the rain has stopped. There's a beautiful lookout spot at the top of this hill. Do you mind if we stop for a little bit?

DRIVER:
Sure. I've been so caught up in the conversation I don't even know where we are anymore.

RIDER:
We are about five miles from the border.

The driver pulled over, shut off the truck and peered at the road behind us. As he climbed out of the truck, a feeling of undeniable reassurance rushed over him.

DRIVER:
I'm more than five miles away from wherever I started.

DISTRACTIONS

We arrived at the top of the hill and
sat down on the damp ground.

RIDER:
Sometimes on my way to work I lose all concept of time
and space. My head is in another place but my body is
present to steer and navigate. I'll get to the office and realize
I don't remember anything about the commute.

DRIVER:
I know what you mean. I don't even have to think about
driving anymore. It's just a habit.

RIDER:
We have become so conditioned to the route it's as if we're
numb to the action of driving.

DRIVER:
Yeah, exactly! I'm usually distracted by other things like
what I have to get done that day or problems at home. I
don't even think about the stoplights I hit on the way.

RIDER:
So we want to retrain ourselves to pay attention to the
signals and not be internally distracted.

Let's sit on that bench over there. I want to show you
something.

He took a deep breath, exhaling as if he didn't want to release the air he had taken in.

Miles and miles of serene land stretched out before us.

DRIVER:
Wow, you were right. This view is incredible!

RIDER:
Places like this help me relax and remind me to pause and be present in the moment.

DRIVER:
I don't get to places like this very often. It feels like there's always too much to do. Our family usually vacations at the beach for 10 days every summer, but that's about the only real relaxation I get during the year.

RIDER:
I bet that feels amazing.

It does. So amazing I never want it to end. But eventually you have to snap back to reality.

RIDER:
I know the feeling. Our family used to do the same thing. Then I decided I didn't want to live a unfulfilled life for 50 weeks just to feel amazing two weeks out of the year.

DRIVER:
So what did you do? Move to the beach?

RIDER:
I wish. Colorado would be my choice.

Instead, I trained myself to be fully present in every moment, good or bad.

DRIVER:
How did you do that?

RIDER:
Close your eyes.

His brow furrowed as he glanced over at me.

DRIVER:
No.

RIDER:
Why not?

DRIVER:
Because this is the part in horror movies where I make the mistake of trusting a hitchhiker with my life.

RIDER:
Just trust me. I'm going to teach you how I started. Close your eyes.

He hesitated, slowly turning forward; his eye lashes barely touched his face as he closed his eyes.

DRIVER:
OK. But for the record, I think you're crazy.

RIDER:
I am. Crazy about feeling alive.

Now, with your eyes closed, inhale a slow, deep breath. Feel the air enter your body through your nostrils and feel your belly expand. Now exhale slowly, feeling the air leave your body.

Next, turn your attention to your muscles. With your mind, scan your body from head to toe and settle on a muscle that is flexed or feels tight. Release the tension in that muscle.

DRIVER:
You're going to put me to sleep.

RIDER:
Relaxed is more of what we're going for.

Now turn your attention externally. Feel that breeze?

> A mild wind brushed past us, hushing any
> reservations that hung in the air.

DRIVER:
Yeah, it feels great. It's giving me goose bumps.

RIDER:
That's great awareness!

He felt them trickle down his spine and to his legs, where his hair stood straight up.

Breathe in again and exhale slowly. Soak in this moment.

Now open your eyes. Take in this view. The sunlight piercing through the clouds. The rainbow circling the horizon. See the drops of water on the blades of grass?

> He opened his eyes. It took him a moment to
> adjust to the light sky.

DRIVER:
Where are you going with this?

RIDER:
I consider myself to be a very driven person, but even in the midst of my ambition I want to look at that blade of grass

and find the beauty in this moment. I want to feel myself relax and let down.

That's what the beach is for.

RIDER:
And we can have that beach experience every day of the year, even in the midst of the stressful business meeting or chaos at home.

DRIVER:
I don't know what your beach experiences are like but mine aren't very productive. You know the song? "Ass in the sand, cold beer in my hand."

RIDER:
I know the song, and my days in Colorado are like that. What keeps us from experiencing that the other 50 weeks of the year is emotional awareness. We have blocked up our ability to be present with our feelings.

DRIVER:
Our feelings? Those just get in the way. You can't be emotional and be successful in my line of work. We make goals and go after them. It's that simple.

RIDER:
Most driven achievers often pursue their craft with a lot of passion and intensity. They push through to the goal. If you're constantly pushing through life then you never learn how to be fully present. You only learn to numb out. You make the drive but you don't know how you got to your destination.

At some point there will be a reckoning. You will be forced to reconcile all of the emotions you've been stuffing down.

He squirmed.

DRIVER:

This seems really squishy and touchy feely. Everything I have learned in business has said you can't give a lot of credence to your feelings because they'll force you to make bad decisions.

RIDER:

I was taught the same thing. Now we seem to be taught the opposite; to feel whatever you feel and act on it. If you feel like raging, rage on. No one has the right to tread on you. Make them pay for what they have done. It's reality TV culture that is dominated by emotions and turns everything into a volatile relationship.

If you deny your emotions, like we were taught, then you rigidly push through and become a worse version of yourself. You lose the ability to feel the temperature of the room and bring the leadership that the situation needs.

We need to learn how to feel what we feel without being dominated by our emotions or denying them.

> He folded his arms, digging his foot in a patch of dirt on the ground.
>
> The breeze he had felt moments ago seemed far away.

DRIVER:

So we aren't supposed to ignore our feelings and we aren't supposed to act out on our feelings. What are we supposed to do when we feel them?

RIDER:

Pay attention to them. Emotions are momentary. They are going to pass. Learn to reinterpret their signals. This is how you avoid being reactionary. You can feel multiple, polar emotions at once and not be dominated by either extreme.

I can feel excited and scared at the same time.

Right before I give a presentation at work I usually feel my heart race and adrenaline kick in. A false interpretation of that tells me there is danger around the corner. I need to run away and take cover.

Instead I reinterpret the emotion as excitement. I felt that same heart pounding adrenaline rush before the first date I had with my wife.

By leaning into the very thing we instinctively want to ignore, we position ourselves to flip potentially crippling emotions until they ease into a positive momentum.

DRIVER:
So you're hitting the pause button before things spiral out of control?

RIDER:
That's a great way to put it. We have to be fully present with ourselves before we can learn to figure out what's broken in the story we are telling ourselves. When you are fully aware you will notice that grimace on your face and feel yourself kicking into gear to be upset. Then you'll retrace the steps and pinpoint what caused the change in course.

When you see this in yourself you start to recognize it in others too. You notice the facial mannerisms of your co-workers, the tone in their voice or the beads of sweat on their nose. You recognize something that feels threatening to them and you can learn to speak to that.

DRIVER:
It feels like you're talking about becoming some kind of Jedi master.

RIDER:
You will stand out because you'll be speaking at a root level while everyone else is managing surface-level responses.

DRIVER:
Why don't more people grasp this? You could really develop some influential interpersonal skills.

RIDER:
Most people are numb. They are driving mindlessly. Over time there is no awareness.

Do you see that tree over there?

> A large oak tree sat beside us.

> Its long branches grew outwards as if craving something just out of reach.

> Dark green moss was creeping up onto the trunk leading into a dark, round hole.

When my brother and I were kids there was a tree like that in the neighborhood. We dared each other to stick our hands in the hole and see how long we could leave it in there.

The catch was that the tree was infested with black ants. After a minute our hands were covered in them. It wasn't long before they were completely numb. Once we lost all feeling we pulled our hands out of the tree, shook off the ants and let the feeling come back to them.

DRIVER:
That's disgusting.

> I laughed when I saw the look of utter disgust on his face.

RIDER:

I still can't believe we did that. But most of us are subjecting ourselves to a similar demise every day.

Our hands were a testament to the reality that a hundred bites in a small amount of time had a numbing effect. It was as if from all those bites, our hands simply died.

We incur these small bites throughout our days: a misunderstanding boss, an annoying team member, a crazy client, an exasperated spouse. A hundred problems overwhelming us.

DRIVER:

Yeah, but all of that is just part of life. You figure out how to deal with it and keep moving.

RIDER:

How do you deal with a day like that?

DRIVER:

Well, I usually go home and turn on the TV. It's a good way to decompress from the day.

RIDER:

It's like taking a warm bath. We soak in the saturation of the story a TV program provides.

DRIVER:

I'm more of a shower guy, but I guess that's true.

RIDER:

Story is fueling the emotional survival of modern society. It is the companion that doles out relief from prisons to nursing homes and our everyday lives. But it's just an escape. It doesn't actually enhance who we are. It's an empty return.

DRIVER:
So what should I do with an empty day?

RIDER:
You hit the pause button. You don't get caught up in what is or isn't happening in your work or relationships because good and bad things will always happen. Instead, pay attention to what is going on inside you with regard to who you are.

Pull your hand out of the tree and shake off the ants until the feeling returns. As you do that you will notice the pain points and what you need to pay attention to.

Pay attention to when you need to lean over and give your wife a hug after a fight, or when you need to reinterpret a tense interaction with your child. Notice when you need to follow up a short, directional email with an in-person interaction to provide context.

DRIVER:
You really think watching TV is keeping us from all that?

RIDER:
I think most people have built in daily habits and routines to distract them from the present moment, especially when the moment calls attention to their pain or vulnerability. They don't consciously do it but it's the rhythm they build to keep themselves going. Future plans are constructed to avoid dealing with present problems. Living detached from the moment they watch their performance and become their own worst critic.

If they learn to just be where they are, they can see the failure, feel the pain, hear the disappointment and then allow those feelings to open up an appreciation for growth.

Accepting the sorrows, the troubles, the defeats wake us up to the present moment. You learn about yourself and wake up to the reality that you are growing and changing. You are not who you once were.

He looked forward again.

His eyes scanned the horizon, perhaps in hopes of seeing the breeze making its way back.

DRIVER:
You find a lot of value in problems and negativity, don't you?

RIDER:
I find a lot of value in growing. When I'm secure in my identity, regardless of what is happening around me, I can use present problems to inspire growth within myself. I understand that mistakes or problems are not an attack on my identity but a removal of distraction.

He shook his head and shrugged.

DRIVER:
I would rather sit on a beach for 50 weeks a year.

RIDER:
Last spring my kids were begging me to take them to the park on the first sunny day of the season. I took off work a little early, grabbed my reclining lawn chair and took them to the park. I'm laying in my chair, headphones in, favorite music soothing me into a Zen moment.

We weren't there for more than 10 minutes when my kids wanted to go back home because they were too hot. I didn't want to leave because I was in this amazing moment. But I was outnumbered so I took them back home.

DRIVER:
Kids always win.

RIDER:
So true.

Trying to be flexible, I decided I would just recreate the moment on the deck at home. But my wife was on the deck and she wanted to talk. I wanted my Zen moment, but I also wanted to be available to her so we talked. It was pollen season and my allergies kicked in to full gear. I was sneezing unbearably. My Zen moment was officially ruined.

> Sitting back against the bench, his voice was reminiscent of many similar experiences.

DRIVER:
I know that experience. When all you want to do is kick back and relax for a minute but no one else wants to let you do that.

RIDER:
It stressed me out. But I paid attention to that feeling and leaned into it. What I learned in that moment is that I will never be as peaceful or stress-free as I want.

We can't recreate past moments of peace. We can only reattach to the present moment. Be here now. We are never going to have optimal external conditions, but we can recognize internally that what we feel afraid of is not true. We can ground ourselves.

DRIVER:
Ground ourselves? What do you mean?

RIDER:
I mean feel your feet.

DRIVER:
What?

RIDER:

Shrink everything down to a small moment of awareness. Like you did earlier by feeling the breeze across your face. When the pressure is on, when you get nervous, when everything feels like it's falling apart, just feel yourself sitting in the conference room chair.

This makes us resilient and unstoppable in performance because mistakes do not shut us down. All we have is this moment. Life needs us right where we are.

> He planted his feet firmly on the ground.
> An unsure expression spread across his face.

DRIVER:

I'm not really sure what this is supposed to accomplish.

RIDER:

Let me give you some more specific examples. Do you golf?

DRIVER:

Yeah, I golf a little bit. I'm not very good but I like to hack away at the ball.

RIDER:

They say golfers are two shots away from going crazy.

DRIVER:

I can attest to that!

RIDER:

It's only true because we can't let go of the last two shots we missed. They are distractions from being here now, in this present moment. And every bad shot compounds on the next one until it spirals out of control. Clubs go flying and everyone wants to quit.

DRIVER:
Been there, done that. Golf can be one of the most frustrating games.

RIDER:
So next time you're on the course and you hit a bad shot and you feel your frustrations boiling up, hit the pause button. Feel your feet. Close your eyes and feel the breeze across your face. Reattach to the present moment.

DRIVER:
And then what? My ball is still lying behind a tree.

RIDER:
There's no magic formula here. The way I see it, you have two options. You can stand over the ball thinking, "I'm a terrible golfer. Why am I even out here? I should have stayed home. I'm a failure."

Or you can stand over the ball, fully present, taking account of all the variables with a clean filter, and give it your best swing. Maybe this is one of those times where you relax into the present moment and land it on the green.

DRIVER:
That's almost inspiring.

RIDER:
It is inspiring! This isn't hype. It's every day life.

It's the entrepreneur who resists the temptation to chase future growth to be present in the current moment. Instead of ignoring present realities he takes time to set up a healthy financial system even when finances are low because he knows it will be beneficial in the long run.

Think of the professional who's ambitiously building a career she may not even enjoy. Instead of numbing out to the pain of that emptiness or taking it out on people she loves, she sits with it. She considers what changes she needs to make. She faces the pain of how the ambition has eroded who she is because it wasn't coupled with awareness. She never learned how to be future focused and present engaged. Instead, consider what it's like to be a person with ambition and presence; to be driven but also able to downshift into a present state of, "I am here now. Nothing can threaten my dignity. I am enough. I'm not missing out."

DRIVER:
Those big breakthrough moments don't seem to happen for me. I'm not a super creative or inspiring guy. I just roll up my sleeves and get the job done.

RIDER:
Not every moment is going to produce euphoria. The objective is to be present with each moment and keep showing up as if it might be one of those times when you feel alive and connected.

You've had these moments. It may have been small and it may have been a long time ago. It's time to stop disregarding them.

He gave a nod, a smile escaping from his lips.

DRIVER:
I just remembered something. I think I was about 11. I was playing in the woods with my brother and we had built a fort. Hours passed and it was if we were lost in a world of our own. When Mom eventually called for us to come inside, it felt like she was calling us back to another life; one we had left behind. I never wanted that moment to end.

RIDER:
That's a great example! What were the circumstances surrounding that moment?

DRIVER:

I had a machete for chopping branches. He had his BB gun. There were no roles to fulfill. Our only responsibility was to play.

RIDER:

That's great information. Go there in your mind's eye. What do you see? What do you hear? What do you feel? Deepening this experience can help you position yourself to find center in chaotic moments. Any time you are having trouble getting to a place of fully present, fully engaged, recall a moment when you didn't feel any fear of fitting in or performing or having what it takes.

DRIVER:

Is this is how you can have a beach experience every day?

RIDER:

Exactly. The highest performers know how to recover under pressure. We will never be free from all pressure. If you solve all of today's problems, the solutions will just create a batch of new problems tomorrow. Instead, we focus our energy on being here, now.

Even in the painful parts, the pain teaches us, it's a removal of distraction and false threats. Our brains still think we're in the cave. From an evolutionary standpoint we are afraid that if we're not liked by the community and contributing the way others think we should, then we won't get our share of the wooly mammoth meat. Those are false fears that distract. Pain wakes us up to what really needs to be seen. It directs our focus to where we need to be fully present. We engage each moment like this might be one of those times where all the fear is gone and existence has a purity difficult to put into words.

We sat in silence for a little while longer.
He looked back at the oak tree; a breeze rustled its green leaves.

DRIVER:
I know we need to get back on the road, but given the conversation we just had, do you mind if we just soak in this sunset a little while longer.

RIDER:
Fantastic idea! Soak it in with all of your senses so we can tap into this moment later.

BLIND

We sat for a little while longer.
He held his gaze with the sunset until he began to fidget.

DRIVER:
Are you ready to get back on the road?

RIDER:
Yeah, I'm ready if you are. I think we're getting close.

DRIVER:
Close for you. I have a long way to go.

RIDER:
You don't live close to here?

DRIVER:
I do, but I'm not going back.

I slowed my pace, my brow furrowing at his answer.

RIDER:
You're not?

DRIVER:
There's nothing that excites me about that life anymore.

RIDER:
You seem like such a motivated person. Aren't there goals you are still trying to reach?

DRIVER:

Yeah, I guess there are. Things used to be so hopeful and full of promise. I was accomplishing so much at work and with my family. Now I feel like everything's stalled out.

RIDER:

Most things start out with a sense of wonder. The hope and promise you're talking about. That typically spurs into bravado when you increase your intensity and really go after the goal.

DRIVER:

I know that feeling. I've always been that way. Now I just feel depressed. I've never felt this way before. I've never struggled so much just to get out of bed in the morning to get the day started.

RIDER:

It's called disillusionment.

DRIVER:

So it gets better after this?

> As we reached the bottom of the hill I heard the jingle of keys as the driver reached into his pocket.

RIDER:

Not to be the bearer of bad news, but it usually gets worse. Next comes the despair.

DRIVER:

Splendid. Another good reason to not go back.

RIDER:

Running away won't solve anything. You'll still cycle through the same phases in your next venture.

> The old Ford lurched forward.

He switched on the radio and moments later switched it off.

DRIVER:
How do you get the wonder and magic back then? How do you regain motivation?

RIDER:
You give up trying to find the old motivation.

DRIVER:
I don't understand.

RIDER:
When my kids played Little League softball, I had to fulfill a rotation in the snack shack.

DRIVER:
Oh, I hated snack shack duty!

RIDER:
You know about this responsibility?

DRIVER:
It's the worst! People who can't make up their minds are constantly bugging you, they're paying with sweaty bills and I'm serving lukewarm hot dogs when all I want to do is watch my daughter bat.

RIDER:
I used to show up 20 minutes late to every game just so I could avoid any substitute voluntary duties.

DRIVER:
Now that is genius! You are a veteran softball dad. We used to bring lawn chairs and sit in the outfield. If they really wanted our help they would have to hike around the fence to get us.

RIDER:
This is what happens in the disillusionment and shattering phases.

DRIVER:
We start living off lukewarm hot dogs?

RIDER:
Not always.

We escape the "shoulds".

DRIVER:
The "shoulds"?

RIDER:
Yeah, the "should". We are all faced with surrounding pressures telling us what jobs we should have, what career we should focus on, what we should do to please our parents, what relationships we should and shouldn't have.

Instead of building a life on what we want, we blindly write a story based on what we feel pressure to do.

> He glanced down at the picture of his family.
> Each member, a piece of string woven into a quilt.
> He was afraid of unraveling all he had worked to accomplish.

DRIVER:
I have spent years building this story. How can I possibly change it now?

RIDER:
Spend less time in the snack shacks of your life.

DRIVER:

Are you advising me to start showing up 20 minutes late to work?

RIDER:

I'm not suggesting you get fired. There will still be some things you have to do that you're not passionate about. As much as you can, though, stop saying yes to things you feel outside pressure to engage in. As you move away from the snack shacks of your life, you will gain an awareness and understanding of who you are and what your story is. The desires that have been buried under all the "shoulds" will surface.

DRIVER:

That's going to be hard to start saying no to everything. I'm usually the most ambitious person in the group.

RIDER:

I remember in college playing golf with my buddies. The seventh hole was adjacent to a line of houses. My second shot hooked right over the fence into a backyard. If I did that today, I would probably just grab a new ball and take the stroke penalty. But for a college kid that golf ball is worth a couple boxes of Ramen noodles, so I went after it.

There was a tree stump right next to the fence. I stepped on the stump and launched myself up and over the fence. I didn't realize beforehand that the stump was rotten. It caved in while I jumped up. I had committed my body to clear the fence but my shins lagged behind.

DRIVER:

Ouch! That had to hurt!

RIDER:

It was incredibly painful. That fence left an intimate tattoo across the front of my legs. I remember lying on the ground, looking up at the sky and hearing the laughter from all my buddies.

DRIVER:
That sounds humiliating!

RIDER:
It gets worse. As I'm lying there, patching up the fence tattoo on my shin, one of my buddies walks down the fence line, opens an unlocked gate, strolls right into the backyard and picks up the ball.

DRIVER:
I'm sure they enjoyed that.

RIDER:
The laughter shrieked louder than my throbbing shins.

> He placed a hand on one of his shins as if he could feel the pain radiating up and down his own legs.

RIDER:
This is what so many of us do, though. We don't even know the pressures that are driving us. We get focused on something that's based on a should and we try to launch ourselves from it. But eventually it caves in. We become miserable on the inside because we lose center.

DRIVER:
How did I not see this from the beginning? And why am I just now feeling the effects of it?

RIDER:
The pressure of "should" eventually wears off. That sounds like what is happening for you now. And much of the time the "should" is unspoken. It is the nudging pressure, the unspoken demands of our cultural heritage or our family systems, and the pressure we force upon ourselves. They

block us up from being who we are and living out of our core.

> The driver adjusted his grip on the steering wheel. He eased himself into contemplation regarding his next question.

DRIVER:
What if I'm tired and I don't care?

RIDER:
That's normal. It's not normal to admit it. Whenever we start paying attention to this we notice that we lose old motivations. We think it's burnout but it's something deeper. We're not motivated to relate to our work, our loved ones, or even ourselves the way we used to be. We are afraid to admit that loss of motivation. But you can't regain old motivations. You only find new ones even if it's for existing commitments. Anybody who thinks they regained an old motivation is afraid and zealously props up an old one that will eventually fade away. When you recognize the "should" that is driving your motivation you can start accepting reality. This is how you regain motivation. You stop pretending or powering your way through what isn't really on the inside.

DRIVER:
Everything else I have learned about motivation talks about setting up reward systems for meeting goals. You don't think those are effective?

RIDER:
Do you use reward systems?

DRIVER:
I have used them for myself some and even with my kids, but mostly with my team at work.

RIDER:
How effective are they?

DRIVER:
For me they are usually very effective. My team at work experiences a lot of turnover, but for the most part they work.

RIDER:
They can be effective, but usually only in the short term. You can't manage someone long term to not live from his or her desires. The carrot-stick rewards work on you because they probably match what you desire to do anyway. At work you are motivating your team to do what you want, not taking into account their desires. Eventually they disengage, hence a possible reason for your high turnover rate. There is not enough income advancement, or carrot sticks, to capture their heart and their energy and their passion.

The shallow motivations are sex, money, and power; our innate biological drives, the money that we think will fix our problems and the power that makes us feel validated for who we are. Once we get those we realize they are not enough.

DRIVER:
What else do we need?

RIDER:
One study named three things we need in regards to our work: meaning, mastery and autonomy. We want to be empowered to go after the things we want to do, we want to get to the edge of our abilities, and we want to do something with meaning. Most people never transcend the basic biological drives, power, sex or the golden handcuffs of money. They never accept the reality that they are more than those insecure needs.

DRIVER:
You're saying that's what leaders need to help them do?

RIDER:
The essence of leadership is empowering others to figure out who they are and the contribution they desire to make. Leadership that doesn't empower others is abusive and a waste of influence. Empowering leaders help others find their vision. Unsafe leaders make others fit the vision they've crafted in their head.

DRIVER:
But even these leaders you are calling unsafe get results.

RIDER:
True. But if you don't create a space for desires to surface you will short-circuit the development of people. You can berate someone for not caring enough, but until they learn to stoke their own fire, your efforts as a leader will not be received.

DRIVER:
I think one of my strengths is motivating people. Are you telling me that a leader, or in my case, a boss, isn't responsible for their employee's motivation?

RIDER:
That's right. It doesn't mean you can't motivate others. It sounds like you might be good at motivating others. There's not a clean answer for every situation. It's most important that you create a trajectory where the people under your leadership own the process of developing their own motivation. Then results will take care of themselves.

DRIVER:
What do you do with the people who are motivating themselves toward responsibilities outside their role on the team?

RIDER:

The first question is are they growing with the same vision the organization has? If not, then they are self-selecting off the team. As the leader, you will have to make a change. Maybe the team member is privately struggling with whether they should stay as they discover desires true to who they are. If that's the case, he or she needs to show up to work fully engaged, not giving any reason to be forced out while quickly figuring out the best move to match those desires.

The bigger issue is whether desire matches up with reality. Have you seen American Idol?

DRIVER:

Oh yeah. I think I know where you're going with this. The people at the beginning of the season who don't belong anywhere near a music audition?

RIDER:

Exactly. Part of regaining motivation is acceptance. To begin a process of change in your life you must first accept things as they are. We would rather run from the moment and not allow ourselves to pay attention to it, but we need to learn to lean into where we are now.

The house we just moved into has a great backyard with a patio, but I don't have a grill or patio furniture yet.

DRIVER:

That's brutal. I love to grill. It's one of my favorite ways to unwind.

RIDER:

Me too!

If I can't face the reality of an empty patio, I will follow the hype mentality and pretend that it's something it isn't. Or I will become rigid and refuse to enjoy any of it until the whole backyard is finished.

Instead, I accept things as they are. I can enjoy it where it is at this moment.

> The driver nodded out the window at the evening sky, as if motioning to a memory or a familiar face.

DRIVER:
This sounds like what we were talking about at the lookout point. Be here, now; fully present.

RIDER:
That's right!

DRIVER:
But a lot of what keeps me going is the future vision. In your case I would be motivated to finish the backyard because of what it would feel like to grill and eat outside in the springtime.

RIDER:
So we learn to live in the tension of enjoying what it is in this moment, while also knowing we want to grow. We live future-focused and present-engaged. This way we aren't blindly focused on the goal. We can enjoy the process along the way. I may not know exactly how we will get the backyard finished but acknowledging that it's not finished yet is the first step. With the next step, something will change.

DRIVER:
Just take it one step at a time.

RIDER:
That's right.

A pipe burst in our house a while back and flooded the

basement. I walked downstairs and felt my feet slosh in water. At the time I was working 12-hour days to get a business off the ground. Then I finished my day circling our basement feeling at a complete loss.

DRIVER:
Wow. I think I would cry if I walked home to that.

> I nodded, looking down at my shoes that had gone from soaked to damp from river water.

RIDER:
I definitely felt a hot tear flush into my eye. I didn't have the energy to deal with that.

DRIVER:
So what did you do?

RIDER:
I picked up one toy and moved it.

Then I picked up the next toy and moved it.

One toy after another and a couple hours later I was hoisting carpet through the basement window.

> He put his hand out, the breeze from the air conditioner rushing over his skin.

DRIVER:
One step at a time.

RIDER:
I didn't have the energy to tackle that entire project, but I did have the energy to take the right next step.

Herculean strength doesn't change things as much as what

you do with the 10,000 small choices life throws at you every day.

And the first choice is to acknowledge and accept the way things are. "It's OK that I'm like this. It's OK that I'm in this place."

DRIVER:
Sometimes it's not OK that you're like this or that you're in this place.

RIDER:
Pressuring yourself isn't effective long term. How you move forward is key. Self-acceptance is crucial so in your pursuit of change you're not running from who you really are. Fear-based change is just another prison.

The better approach is to say, "It's OK that I'm like this. It's not OK for me to stay in this situation." This separates personhood from performance.

DRIVER:
I've always heard, "You can tell someone's character by what comes out when they're under pressure. Like a shaken cup, what is inside will spill out."

RIDER:
The hardships of life don't show you who you are. How you respond to the hardships shape you. Life is more about who you are becoming than what you achieve. So you fell down. So you handled it poorly. Will you take the next right step?

DRIVER:
Aren't the accomplishments important too? I mean, isn't that what we're always striving for?

RIDER:
It's OK to celebrate wins in our mission or with the

community we are building. That's living present-engaged. Acknowledge that you poured a lot of energy and effort into something and you stretched the limits of your abilities and you did it all with people you enjoy. Celebrate that.

Who we want to become drives the future focus.

DRIVER:
I guess I don't understand this future focused piece. When I accomplish one goal, my focus is on the next.

RIDER:
It's fine to set new goals and aim for new benchmarks. Who you want to become is the subterranean force that moves you each day, in the small moments and through the adversity. It is the resiliency to keep going, the toughness to not cave under pressure.

DRIVER:
It seems so vague; who you want to become. I want to become president of our company.

RIDER:
What kind of president do you want to be? What kind of dad do you want to be? What kind of husband?

Imagine the end of your life. All the people who love you are gathered at a memorial service in your honor. There's a giant picture of you with some markers. Everyone writes one word to describe you. What would the three most common words be?

After a long pause the driver responded softly.

DRIVER:
I've never really thought about that.

RIDER:

For me, I want to be a fully present dad, I want the company I lead to be generous, and I want my work team to be adventurous. As those descriptors guide my everyday choices, they shape who I am becoming in each of those three arenas. When lived out, it is the full, unobstructed expression of who I am.

DRIVER:

That's a really inspiring goal.

RIDER:

It is the future vision, the guiding light of who I'm trying to become. I'm not so future-oriented that I'm tight, rigid and can't relax and enjoy the moment. At the same time I'm not lost in the moment without the guiding light.

DRIVER:

And all of this is supposed to make me think it's a better idea to go back home? I think I would rather start from scratch.

RIDER:

I think if you re-engage with the life you have built you will find a new expression of who you are. You can let go of the dead motivation. You don't have to prop yourself up anymore or prove something you don't believe to be true. You can start a new exciting chapter.

DRIVER:

I feel like I have a long way to go with so much baggage to clean up.

RIDER:

It won't happen over night. You will have to stand in a dark middle phase before there is something new to grab onto. But this is where growth starts. You find one small moment that can inspire you to the next, all while feeling alive in this moment.

BEHAVIOR

The evening sky of orange and blue had faded quickly into a black sheet, the moon and stars its only source of light. We traveled on.

RIDER:
Tell me about your family. Looking at that picture, it's easy to tell that your kids are adorable.

DRIVER:
They are…most of the time. My son is the youngest. He's a pretty shy kid but he's great. So smart and creative. I love hanging out with him. We go to sporting events together and he helps me with the yard work. Those are some of my favorite moments.

RIDER:
That sounds great. I bet he enjoys those experiences too.

> The driver stared down at his son's face for a moment and nodded to himself.

DRIVER:
I hope he does.

My daughter is ambitious like me. She is so smart and personable. She's going to be president of a company someday. She can be a bit of a troublemaker, but look at that smile. How can you get mad at that?

RIDER:
I know how that goes. I have three daughters myself. Melt your heart.

DRIVER:
What are they like?

RIDER:
Three breathing reminders to be here, now. Every parent feels urges to power up or hide because of their fear. And I have three little humans that impact me more than I could have anticipated. My 12-year-old recently helped me see something I would not have noticed in someone else until I was 30.

DRIVER:
Really? How?

RIDER:
One night at dinner my wife gave some direction to the kids that I didn't agree with. It wasn't a big disagreement. It was so small I didn't even register it as being a disagreement. Then it happened. My wife said, "When you disagree with my parenting, you raise your eyebrows. I don't appreciate the way you express your disagreement." Then my daughter spoke up, saying, "Yeah and you let out a deep breath."

DRIVER:
That's amazing! They have you pegged!

> I threw my hands up in the air with a smirk across my face.

RIDER:
It's awful. I can't get away with anything!

The crazy part is as soon as they called me out at dinner I

felt this powerful internal urge to defend myself. I wanted to explain it away by listing all the reasons why I raise my eyebrows.

DRIVER:
No way they would have bought that.

RIDER:
Not a chance!

DRIVER:
So what did you do? You were exposed!

RIDER:
Like when the dentist is digging in your mouth and knows you haven't been flossing. I felt so vulnerable. Then I decided that's exactly what I needed to be in that moment. I just needed to be wrong.

> The driver paused and an unsure silence hung between us.

DRIVER:
You fessed up to it?

RIDER:
I decided I wasn't going to pretend. I was going to be vulnerable.

DRIVER:
How did that work?

RIDER:
Great! Pretending drains energy. Vulnerability gives energy.

If I had worked them over to prove something that wasn't true, they would have felt the insincere nature of it. I would have pushed them away.

DRIVER:
How did they respond when you admitted it?

RIDER:
Everyone at the table laughed. It turned a tense conversation into a bonding moment.

DRIVER:
That's great. Now you're going to have to supplement something else for raising your eyebrows.

RIDER:
You're right. They know me too well!

Recently my kids had come from the pool, showered, and then went back outside to start playing and were running around the yard. I opened the window and went into lecture mode. You know when you string four or five sentences together to pressure your kids into conforming?

DRIVER:
Been there, done that.

RIDER:
Of course my kids replied, "Dad, this is awesome. When you go into lecture mode you have deeply intrigued us with what you're saying and we want to change immediately."

> The driver peered over at me, but this time his eyebrows went up.

DRIVER:
They said what?

RIDER:
I'm kidding. They really said: "Dad, why are you stressed?"

My fear about how the evening might go was keeping me

internally distracted. I was more concerned with future shower routines and implications for evening plans than their present fun.

Do you have any tells that your family picks up on?

DRIVER:
My wife says she knows if I had a bad day at work as soon as I walk into the house.

RIDER:
How does she notice?

DRIVER:
She says I'm tense and barely say "Hi'" to her and the kids. I walk in and launch directly into chores or whatever needs to happen that night at home.

RIDER:
I used to do the same thing. Now I remind myself to check the pulse before completing the task.

DRIVER:
What do you mean?

RIDER:
My natural instinct is to focus on the task that needs to be completed. Whether I'm coming home, arriving at work, leading a meeting, or grabbing coffee with a potential client, I tend to jump right into the to-do list.

The better approach is to hit the pause button. Check the pulse first. Check in relationally before moving to the task. I watch them and try to be present with them, try to make them feel comfortable.

DRIVER:
How do you do that?

RIDER:

I watch their body language and listen to them speak and try to match them. If they are uptight and tense, I'm not going to sit back and kick my feet up like nothing is wrong. If they're language is addressing how they feel, I'm going to match that. I'm not going to say, "I see you," or "I hear you." I'm going to share a story where I felt something similar. If they're telling me a story and say, "Do you see what I'm saying?" then I will affirm and say, "I see what you're saying." And if they ask a question I won't get distracted into telling my story. I'll flip it back and ask them because there's something they want to share. All questions are self-revealing. This is true even for seemingly mundane questions.

> He sat back in his seat and scratched his head.
> We were nearing a stop sign and he eased onto his
> brakes, a noticeably smoother transition on his
> part.

DRIVER:

All this time you have been talking about being authentic and your true self. Now this sounds a bit fake.

RIDER:

There is nothing wrong with using a persona from time to time. It's valuable in growing important relationships, but it needs to be authentic.

There's a difference between who I am and the roles I fulfill. I am a husband but that isn't the sum total of who I am. My roles don't define me.

I like to think about all my roles along the lines of modes. There's three meta-roles or modes I want to be able to move in and out of as the situation demands. I call these empathy, sage, and leader. There is a time to be sensitive and present, a time to issue a warning or to advise, and a time to be the sacrificial leader. Moving in and out of these different relational roles with fluidity has opened up my ability to be present in many more situations. Most people are rigidly stuck in one of those meta-roles falsely believing that's just who they are.

DRIVER:
How do you know when it's authentic and when you're faking it?

RIDER:
Awareness is key. When we have certainty in who we are, we can live in the tension of who we are and who we need to be in this moment. I can tend to be a leader and give direction but the moment may need more storytelling or a sensitive presence. Without awareness of who we are and what the situation needs we will remain stuck relationally. We think we have to maintain a certain role to defend who we insecurely believe we are. As a result, we serve the image of our insecure identity. We become fused to a mask that we think defines who we are. We start pretending.

DRIVER:
You've talked a lot about awareness.

RIDER:
It is the first step in understanding who you are and how experiences are shaping you. Performance addicted people live outside of themselves, watching their performance with harsh judgments. Awareness of the fear and pain helps you become congruent, learning who you are and living grounded in your body, aware of your emotions and authentic in your relationships.

DRIVER:
There you go with that fear talk again.

RIDER:
It is the hidden driver of distracted living.

Let me explain.

Experiences shape your brain, thus they shape you. A thousand small events and a few big events have happened to form who you are and the triggers that set you on fire. All of these moments, big or small, either reinforce who you are or diminish who you are. Since your brain is constantly being shaped by these experiences, you have to pay attention to the framework through which you engage them. Your brain is processing everything through identity. The more aware you are, the more you understand that bad reactions are built on false threats. If you don't reframe these moments then your work and your relationships will be driven by fear, shame, and insecurity. You become a worse version of yourself.

The driver reached up to adjust his rearview mirror.

DRIVER:
I once read an example about how experiences affect the brain. The example was a person arriving at work and being over-celebrated like it was her 40th birthday. Everyday they threw a party just because she was there and she felt really good about going to work.

A different person was berated when he arrived. "Why are you here? I can't believe you would even come." All of this disgust was directed towards him. I guess the weight of that negative experience would burden him long after that one day. He would need a month of the woman's experience of celebration to relax and feel welcomed again.

RIDER:
That's a great example! The brain is constantly reaching back for patterns. Past experiences shape our present response. If you want power over your present response, you need a powerful experience that helps you learn security in who you are. You can take control of this by

learning to harness the flow of your brain so you can calm down and feel secure.

DRIVER:
Are you talking about mediation?

RIDER:
Sure. That's one method. Like we did at the scenic lookout stop. I've also helped people leverage the power of their imagination. However you do it, it is the pathway to feeling secure.

DRIVER:
I've heard about monks and religious folks using mediation, but not in business leadership.

RIDER:
This is why mainstream self-help exhausts us. It tries to force us into a new baseline or default setting. Forcing does not work. Instead you rewire the brain's responses by relaxing into a new brilliance. You learn who you are and the bravado fades away. You learn to recover on the run as you interact with others and lead securely.

> The driver let out a chuckle as he adjusted his rearview mirror.
>
> The highway seemed virtually empty except for a few stray cars ahead of us.
>
> My shoes were starting to dry and the driver's walls that had stood drenched with complacency were now beginning to crumble.

DRIVER:
I feel like you have uncovered the formula to having all the right answers.

RIDER:
Leading and relating to people out of security does not mean you always have the right answers. It means you're not afraid to say, "I don't know." It's me at the dinner table, fessing up to my daughters that I was wrong.

The whole idea is we become more human. People can relate to humans. They can't connect to those who seem to have it all together.

DRIVER:
I remember in college becoming a disciple of an entrepreneurial guru. I read all of his books and listened to his presentations religiously. I wanted to be just like him. Then he came to our school for a seminar. My professor, who was good friends with him, invited me to lunch, just the three of us. During those 90 minutes I learned stuff about my idol I never dreamed would be true. He was just a normal dude, like us, figuring it out as he went. It completely tore down the pedestal I had him on.

RIDER:
How did your feelings toward him change after that?

DRIVER:
I still consumed his material but instead of straining to do everything perfectly and have all the right answers, I felt like I could experiment more and make some mistakes as I got started.

RIDER:
It is our responsibility to deconstruct the pedestal others put us on. It's how we disarm the lie we believe that we can control what others think of us. When we are insecure, we try to control what others think of us so we can manipulate their behavior. Instead, we deconstruct the pedestal they might put us on, reveal that we are human, that we struggle too, and live out of our authentic self.

DRIVER:
How do you deconstruct the pedestal?

RIDER:
You call out your fear.

DRIVER:
You mean to everyone?

RIDER:
Yes.

> He shook his head; resistance made its way into his voice.

DRIVER:
No, no, no. I'm not about to stand in front of our entire company and expose myself that way.

RIDER:
Not everything to everyone. I'm not saying you need to stand in front of the company completely naked.

DRIVER:
Well that's a relief.

RIDER:
I'm talking about being vulnerable in leadership. You lead the way by how you process and respond to the events that are happening to you. People watch how you process the hardship and respond to it. Instead of being a hype artist or shelling out a lot of B.S. you are honest about where you are and how you're growing through it.

DRIVER:
This feels like scary ground to walk on, like we are putting our credibility on the line.

RIDER:

If we aren't putting our credibility on the line, we aren't winning people over. We can't engage them and develop them if they can't see how we are handling different situations. If we are always playing in safe zones we become robots and cause others to interact with a plastic version of who we are rather than the human version.

DRIVER:

I can see how that would be true. There are still things I'm not interested in sharing publicly with our whole company.

> I slid my finger in a circular motion across the dashboard.

RIDER:

Divide your relational circles into three categories: a large public circle, an intermediate circle and a very small tight circle.

In the very small tight circle, express your deepest fears. This is a safe space where you can call out your fear to yourself and to someone else. When you shine light on those dark spaces it brings clarity to who we are and relaxes us into our own brilliance. This may be a very small and safe team you work with or it might be a personal team of support you build around yourself.

Then move out to the intermediate circle. You soften those deepest fears and share enough to deconstruct the pedestal; make them feel like an intimate member of the team and develop them through how you process experiences. No one wants to follow a robot. The people who appear to have it all together usually don't and they end up pushing people away because of their pretenses.

Humanize yourself to the outer circle but you don't have to over share. They also don't want to carry your burdens. You may think it's worth the relief to unload all of your dirty laundry, but all you are doing is burdening others.

DRIVER:
How do you know which circle gets which pieces of information?

RIDER:
Just pay attention. It all depends on where you are and what's happening in the moment. There are times when you need to take it to the gut level with the public circle. Perhaps you need to make a confession to deconstruct a fear that is holding power over you.

If you're unsure, call it out to that very small tight circle. What are you afraid of? What are you scared about the public circle or the intermediate circle finding out? If they knew this about you would it help draw them in to develop and grow them?

Just be sure you test your motives. Some people will share deep fears in the public circle with great intensity to test their followers' commitment. That usually pushes people away.

You can even use a filter for the very small tight circle. If you are putting yourself out there and going after big things, you are going to feel moments of fear every day. You could overwhelm that small circle with every moment of fear. I try to filter it between moments I just need to process through and then more intense moments that I need help.

Does that make sense?

> He exhaled softly as a semi truck passed us.
> His voice was tired.
> It occurred to me how long we had been driving.

DRIVER:
Clear as mud.

I'm kidding. It does make sense. I'm thinking about what that looks like in my life and the people I'm around in the corporate world. Politics are so engrained in my work environment it's really hard to envision showing this weakness and maintaining your stature. Then I've seen people champion vulnerability and take things too far. They lose the trust of senior leadership. I've seen startups lose necessary funding because the founder wanted to be authentic. Hell, I don't want my favorite team's coach to share his struggles in a press conference.

RIDER:
There is a nuance to it. You see it in sports all the time. Coaches are blasted in the media for decisions they make. Talk show hosts rile up the fans to call for the coach to be fired. The discerning coach will have some finesse in his game to decide when to be smart and protect himself. Most will overprotect though and never show that vulnerability until they break down from the pressure.

A lawyer can't confess to a client, "I have no experience making this argument and am terrified of standing in front of the jury for this closing." He needs to share those fears with the very small tight circle. He needs to release control of what the jury will think of him. Then be honest with his client about the odds of the outcome while inspiring hope.

I think you'll find that, in your world, when you humanize yourself to your team, your vulnerability will set you apart from the other insecure leaders. You may set yourself up for attack from competition, but remember you can't control what others think of you. On the other side, you will endear your followers and grow a stronger community. They will start rooting for you. When you pretend to have it all together, they will root against you.

DRIVER:
You're probably right. But it doesn't make it any less scary to do.

RIDER:
I remember cliff jumping into the water last time I came to this river. There was a kid on top of the rock trying to muster the courage to jump. It was about a 25-foot fall to the water.

DRIVER:
Whoa! Brave kid!

RIDER:
Almost. I asked him if he was ready. He said, "Not yet. I'm close, but I'm still scared."

He was waiting to be fear-free before he jumped. The problem is we will never be completely fear-free. If we wait for the perfect conditions, we will never jump.

There were younger kids nearby jumping off a five-foot rock. It was safe. There's nothing scary about that. If we want to remove the fear we can decrease the magnitude of the jump. But if we want to make a big splash, we have to jump while it's still scary.

> We drove on a little bit longer in silence.
> The driver imagined that cliff; water pulsing below, mist falling on his skin.

> I closed my eyes and heard the crashing of waves.
> The smell of river water traced itself along my nostrils. The jump, just beneath my feet.

The best part is when you hit the water. The initial breakthrough shocks the body a bit but you come out of it feeling so alive. You'll want to jump again. This whole process of awareness is about waking up to the pain and the joy.

I opened my eyes.

This, is feeling alive.

ACCEPTED

DRIVER:
I've been meaning to ask you, what are on your feet?

> I propped my right foot up on the opposite knee
> and pointed down at the shoe.

RIDER:
These are "zero drop" shoes. The idea is that the feet don't need angled support but instead should hit the ground with no drop in the foot's sole. It supports better foot mechanics. Then the wide toe box allows the foot to splay out naturally rather than confining it.

DRIVER:
Weirdest shoes I've ever seen.

RIDER:
Sometimes you just have to fly your freak flag.

> He peered over at me, eyebrows furrowed in
> confusion as if I had just spoken a foreign language.

DRIVER:
Do what?

RIDER:
Fly your freak flag.

We all have something that makes us weird. For me, it's footwear and a host of other things. I know my thoughts about footwear aren't mainstream, but it's my thing and I embrace it.

DRIVER:
There is a guy in our office that wears a hideous plaid sports coat every Friday. I swear he is only doing it to get attention.

RIDER:
Some people act out in response to the insecurity they feel. They need to be seen and noticed. But if you are truly living out of your authentic self and it's overflowing into your relationships, then fly your freak flag unashamed.

DRIVER:
I'm going to be honest with you, I have no interest in being the weird neighbor.

RIDER:
We can't control what others think of us. You might be the weird neighbor because you don't stand out. Again, people relate to humans. The idiosyncrasy that sets you apart is the thing that makes you more human. People are attracted to that.

DRIVER:
I remember tight rolling my jeans in junior high so I could hang with the cool kids. It was so uncomfortable, and I felt like a fool. I was willing to try anything to sit at their lunch table.

RIDER:
Did it work?

DRIVER:
They still laughed me off the table. I looked just like them but still couldn't get into their clique.

RIDER:
We're all trying to break into a party that isn't ours.

DRIVER:
I never tried going to the parties. I couldn't even get to the lunch table!

> I let out a hearty laugh.
> His austere expression faded.
> Traces of a grin were all that remained.

RIDER:
No, no. We are insecurely trying to be accepted by a group. Rather than build the party we want to join, we try to break into someone else's party.

DRIVER:
Oh, I understand what you're saying. There are some groups that would be advantageous to be a part of though, whether it's to increase your influence, spread your market share or get a deal finalized.

RIDER:
If you're trying to break into a party, you will constantly be distracted. You try to change and coerce your way into a space that you think will make you whole. That space won't fix all your problems. It won't make you live out of the best version of who you are. You will spend the rest of your life proving or hiding to live up to norms that are not an authentic expression of who you are. Eventually you will become bitter and frustrated because they can't give you what you really need.

DRIVER:
How do you know if you're trying to break into a party or if it's really the party you belong to?

RIDER:

Are you giving something to them or trying to get something from them?

When you're trying to break into a party, your focus is on what they can give you. At the surface level you think this new party will give you the money, influence, accolades or power you need. At a deeper level this goes back to our earlier conversations. Everyone is looking for comfort because they feel fear about who they are. They want to know they are secure, safe, worthy, noticed, loved, needed, cared for, and known. As you build your own party you ask yourself, "What do I have to give and who can I give it to?" You give to others what you're looking for in belonging.

DRIVER:

That reminds me of my son two summers ago. He was saving money to buy a new bike. There was a landscaping business making the rounds through our neighborhood and he thought he could do the same kind of work. He knocked on doors in the neighborhood asking if they needed any work done that he could be paid for. Very few people took him up on it. His ultimate goal was only to get paid.

During the first snowfall of winter I told him to take the shovel and ask the neighbors if he could shovel their driveway. With no agreement on payment or anything, he just shoveled driveways. It turned out the neighbors were even more generous. The neighbors showed their appreciation and he earned enough money that winter to buy a new bike.

RIDER:

Love it! One of the most common mistakes we make is that we try to keep a wide range of options open, flirting with all of them rather than focusing on one area with clarity. Take the options off the table. Serve a specific group of people. Let it grow from there.

Your son may not be able to attract all of the landscaping business in the neighborhood, but he could become the go-to guy for snow shoveling. Neighbors will be turning away bigger companies because of the impact he makes.

The driver paused as he made a swift lane change.

DRIVER:
This probably held back the last company I worked for. We were trying to offer a dozen different products that were of average quality, but none of them excelled. No one really knew what was our specialty.

RIDER:
It's a fear of commitment. We are afraid that if we commit we will lose who we are. The fear is, "What happens if it doesn't work out?"

We don't learn more about who we are in the absence of commitments. We find ourselves in the presence of commitments because it challenges us. It exposes motives and we learn beautiful things about the party we are building.

DRIVER:
How does it expose motives?

RIDER:
This shows up in relationships a lot. When we decide to get married or start a family, it narrows our party, takes options off the table. It's a big commitment. Within that commitment you start to learn what you can give to the relationship and what you're trying to get out of it.

When I first met my wife's parents I noticed her dad helped with the dishes after meals. It registered for me that doing the dishes would be expected of me once we got married because that was a norm in my wife's household.

I used to hate doing the dishes, but I want to grow and I know serving helps me do that, but even now my motives get confusing. When I'm afraid I'm losing myself in the presence of this commitment, I seek to get something from it. As I'm loading the dishwasher I will clank them together and make a lot of noise, hoping my wife will notice me doing the dishes. I want acknowledgement and celebration. I want to receive something from her rather than give something to her.

DRIVER:
That's funny. I was at the coffee shop last week and wanted to leave a tip because they had been especially pleasant that week. There was a jar on the counter clearly labeled "TIPS" but I asked the clerk if that was the tip jar before dropping my money in it. Hearing you tell these stories, I'm sure I was looking for recognition for my generosity.

RIDER:
You're probably right, George Costanza.

DRIVER:
I guess when you are trying to build your own party there are still things you have to do even if you don't enjoy them.

RIDER:
Absolutely. It comes down to giving people what they need. But you can learn to enjoy going about some of those activities. Now when I'm in the kitchen putting dishes away, I listen to music.

DRIVER:
Okay. That makes sense. But how do you recognize what you have to give to help build that party?

RIDER:
Recognize what you want others to think about you. Give that away to others.

I want to be celebrated for who I am and what I do. I want my wife to notice when I do the dishes and I want her to celebrate me for that. Instead of doing the dishes to get something from her, I learn to do the dishes whether it's noticed or not. Then I give what I want to others. I celebrate the people around me for who they are and what they do. That's the kind of party I want to be a part of.

DRIVER:
It comes back to motives, doesn't it? And the leader will dictate if it's a healthy motive or unhealthy.

RIDER:
Exactly. You are the architect of the environment by what comes out of you, oftentimes in the most subtle, mundane moments. You can stress over your kids' behavior and freak out because they aren't doing what you want them to do. You will be building a party based on getting something from them. If they behave well it makes you feel good about who you are as a parent.

Or you can build a party to give something. You can give them empowerment and help them learn who they are and how to bring the fullness of who they are to what they do in life. Instead of stressing over behavior you validate who they are and investigate what's happening in their internal worlds.

DRIVER:
What does this look like at work?

RIDER:
It's about the culture you are trying to build. You shape it through those everyday interactions and the stories you tell. And you test your motives. Do you want your culture to be a certain way because you get something from it? Or are you setting up a culture where you can give who you are?

He wriggled his shoulders; softly shaking his head. In the next lane over a car's brake lights shined and their turn signal flashed.

The driver raised his hand and waved them over.

DRIVER:
It still sounds like you're setting it up to get something out of it. You are positioning it to meet the needs you want rather than the needs of the people in the party.

RIDER:
That's where you start. Test the motives. Why are you doing this and what do you want to get out of it? Are you trying to break into someone else's party? Are you insecurely trying to be accepted by a certain group?

When you're trying to decide what to give away, start by giving what you want. If you want to feel like you belong, give belonging to others. If you want to feel safe, give safety to others. If you want to feel worthy just for who you are or you want your performance celebrated, give that to others.

As the motives become healthier and your community grows from your secure identity, you will shift to build around the needs of the weakest members or those in need of the most development. That's what propels the mission forward.

He let out a sigh.

I sat back in my seat, listening to the wind weaving in between the tires of our car and feeling another objection coming from the driver.

DRIVER:
I understand the idea of building your own party and not trying to be accepted by others, but I don't agree with that

last part. I'm not building around our weakest members. I'm going to run with my best performers.

RIDER:

One of my daughters has a severe allergy to dairy products. So much so, that it has changed the way we eat and stock food in the house. We only eat at vegan restaurants and at home we have almond milk and cashew milk ice cream. Now, I could be a jerk father and bring home delicious ice cream sundaes for everyone and slide her a cup of soy ice cream. But if I am secure in who I am we will build our family rhythm around her needs.

DRIVER:

That makes sense. Of course you aren't going to kick your daughter to the curb. But in business we have goals we are trying to meet. I'm not going to slow those down just because one person can't cut it.

RIDER:

I'm not saying you should slow down. Set the performance standards that will challenge your team and keep them engaged at the edge of their abilities. But set up your team culture to help the weakest develop to where the team is at its highest functioning unit.

If there is one person who can't own up to mistakes and regularly passes blame, how does the culture help her feel safe enough to admit when she is wrong?

If there is a team member who stays on the edge of burnout, how does that culture help her learn to ask for what she needs?

If there is a leader who is constantly chasing the next fantasy and not facing the reality of the data, how does the culture help him calm down and appreciate the small consistent steps to move forward?

Our speed had been deteriorating.
I felt the acceleration beneath my feet.
The driver passed the cars in front of us.

DRIVER:
Sometimes they just need to be fired.

RIDER:
If they are constantly trying to go behind your back
and tear you down then yes, they need to go. But by not
removing the source of dissension you're still building
around the weakest members of the team, the ones who
aren't secure enough to resist that toxic employee.

If you ask enough questions and find out they can't meet
performance goals because their desires pull them in a
different direction then sure, let them fly elsewhere.

If you have processed your own internal motives and decide
your frustration with them is not just because they are
challenging you and making you feel insecure, then maybe
it's time to let them go. You can't lead people well when
you're frustrated at them.

> I paused, peering back at the cars trailing behind
> us.

But not everyone is maliciously trying to bring you down.
What systems do you have in place to discover who
is? What approach do you take to help those who are
interested to grow out of their self-sabotaging behaviors?

These systems are important because one toxic employee
can cause you to spend more energy moving sideways when
you could be investing that energy in the growth of the
business.

> He pursed his lips together.

He could see his heavy office door closing behind an employee.

A stiff conversation would follow.

DRIVER:
That's a really hard conversation to have, to tell someone they aren't measuring up.

RIDER:
It gets really messy when you can't separate personhood from performance.

DRIVER:
What do you mean?

RIDER:
To be a savvy articulate leader you have to be able to communicate the difference between personhood and performance. If you just correct performance it will oftentimes block people up in who they are. They will shut down.

> With my hands I outlined parallel columns running from the roof to my lap.

I envision two columns. Everything I say in this column is related to personhood. "I'm glad you are on our team. I enjoy being around you." Everything in the other column is performance. "Your response to the customers is scaring them away. Let's change that performance."

DRIVER:
At our last employee summit I had to challenge the marketing team to do a better job. Research and development was at an all-time high, the quality of our products was improving, but the marking just didn't seem to be connecting with our target audience. Later I found

out the people in marketing were depressed because they felt like I was on the verge of firing them.

I looked back at him.

He was concentrated on the road, but his mind was far away.

RIDER:
Were you?

DRIVER:
No. I really like the people in that department. They are brilliant, creative thinkers. But they had missed the bull's eye on this new campaign.

RIDER:
As you learn to build around the needs of the weakest members, you will learn to attune to what they hear, not just what you say. You may be venting and think it's coming off as call to change focus or direction. What they hear based on your tone mixed with their insecurity is that they are inadequate. That's when they shut down.

DRIVER:
Wow, it seems so complex and draining. I shouldn't have to spend so much energy on this touchy feely stuff. Let's set the goals, figure out how we're going to get there and go after it. Get your counseling sessions somewhere else.

The driver had found the broken pieces of his wall and was slowly trying to repair the obstructed view he had held onto for so long.

In the midst of a barren highway and the darkness that enveloped us at all sides,

I held the pieces down once more.

RIDER:

You can ignore it if you want, but you will do more harm than good to people in the long term. There is no one in your company who wishes you would be more of a jerk to get them motivated; no one wishes you would power up so they could feel less free to make decisions and bring their creativity.

Think about the party you want to be a part of. If you were a sales person in your company or on the marketing team, how would you want to be led? Give that to them.

When you go home tonight, what kind of father would you want to have? Give that to your kids.

> For the first time in a while, he broke his staring contest with the road.

> We had once been strangers.

> Fleeing, returning.

> I set my sights on the road before us.

Start building the party you want to be a part of.

SELF-SABOTAGE

We pulled onto a rural road. The open skies rolled out before us with patches of stars hanging above the dusty road.

The driver steadied his map on the steering wheel; scanning the winding lines that would lead us to the end of our journey.

DRIVER:
Looks like we are only a few miles from the canoe shop. They're probably open now.

RIDER:
That's great news! Thanks again for giving me a lift. I didn't know how I was going to get back with the boat destroyed and my cell phone ruined from the water.

DRIVER:
No problem. I've really enjoyed the conversation. You have an interesting perspective on life.

RIDER:
Thanks for saying that. I've enjoyed it too. It has reminded me of what has helped me in the past.

There was a brief silence.

The driver set the map on the ground.

DRIVER:
What are you going to do when you get home?

RIDER:
We're actually in the middle of some home renovations so I'll probably spend time on those before the weekend is gone.

DRIVER:
That doesn't sound like much fun. I hate manual labor.

RIDER:
I used to feel the same way.

DRIVER:
I have no handyman skills. My dad tried to teach me but he would just get frustrated because I couldn't do it right.

RIDER:
Sounds like he couldn't give what he didn't have. I'm definitely learning as I go. I remember my first job in college was in concrete construction. I didn't know what I was doing. I'm not even sure how I got the job. I had mowed the lawn growing up but I wasn't especially skilled with a hammer or anything.

My first day on the job they handed me a 16-pound sledgehammer. We had to nail giant spikes into steel frames. One of the supervisors held the spike and told me to drive it into the frame.

>He shook his head and let out a chuckle.
>I, too, was still a little amused at the whole situation.

DRIVER:

This sounds like a disaster waiting to happen.

RIDER:

I was a frail, skinny, weak college freshman. I could barely lift the sledgehammer, much less control where I was swinging. I missed so bad I nearly pulverized the guy's hand.

DRIVER:

Geez! What did he do?

RIDER:

I heard a combination of syllables and words come out of his mouth that the universe has never heard before. He lit me up!

DRIVER:

I bet that was intense!

RIDER:

So intense! I had to learn really fast how to handle that sledgehammer.

DRIVER:

Innovate or die, right?

RIDER:

I guess you could say that. By the end of the summer I adapted and could handle the sledgehammer and figured out how to carry multiple steel frames at once, but it was dangerous in the beginning.

It makes me think of how many times we gloss over developing the parts of us that need to be stronger so we can operate in a way that creates the results we want.

He looked over at me for a moment and then returned to the road, offering some good-natured harassment as if we had been friends for years.

DRIVER:
Everything is a life lesson for you, isn't it?

RIDER:
Every moment is an opportunity for growth. Every time we feel something, it's a clue and a message to who we are, to where we are headed, to something that can grow and change within us. It's a way we can recognize how to build stuff with that hammer rather than repeatedly smash our thumb.

I learned a while ago that I was consistently covering up present concerns to chase the future. It's how I ventured into a business decision that left me on the hook for seven zeros and it's how I justified working too much to impress someone that didn't really value me.

I decided I would stop making self-sabotaging choices. Instead of being distracted by the things that held me back I started living from desire. I learned to replace the distractions with my desires.

DRIVER:
How did you get there?

RIDER:
I think you know how I'm going to respond to that question.

He leaned back in his seat.

If his mind had been traveling before, it had returned.

DRIVER:
Awareness?

RIDER:
That's it. Pay attention and you will notice the times your choices produce results that make you miserable. You may even be able to look back on your life now and recognize a pattern of self-sabotaging choices.

DRIVER:
We recently hired a guy whose references seemed too good to be true. I was leery about hiring him because of that, but he did really well in the interview. Sure enough, six months into it my concerns were validated. In meetings he talked a big game but he consistently failed to develop leaders. He built teams that were dependent on him for every small decision rather than empowering others. He didn't last a year with us.

RIDER:
I've seen that so many times. Leaders are not developed because the team leader feels the stress of being replaceable if they are not needed. They sabotage their future because they are swallowed up in present insecurity. They react to an attack that isn't there.

We have to learn to recognize when we have an unnecessary stress response to a situation. Then we are able to reinterpret it, not as an attack on our dignity, but a removal of distraction. No present circumstance can add or take away from who we are. If we can't navigate the stress of the present moment and see beyond the false threat to our identity we will miss our future potential. We lose the ability to move forward with optimism. Not a naïve, hyped optimism, but an informed optimism. Better to face reality fiercely with an understanding that what is happening right now is not an attack on your dignity. Even though we may interpret it that way initially, we are aware of the real threat, not the false one.

I've started a few businesses and led some turnarounds. Every time it gets hard there's a tendency for my self-talk to ask, "Who do you think you are to attempt this?" At that point I can be distracted or let it stir up the desires for what I want. I can waste energy ruminating over a false threat and miss the real threat where something in my business needs attention. As my kids have aged I have to adjust how I relate depending on what stage they are in. Rather than taking their actions as an attack to my dignity, I pay attention and remind myself I want to have a lifelong adult relationship with them. So I adjust to where they are. My desire to have a lifelong relationship with them is the true desire. Feeling the need to take control because I feel insecure is a distraction. To be an informed optimist is to replace distractions with true desires.

DRIVER:
I have always thought desire was the problem. We are all in it for selfish gain and that's what is causing the conflict. But you sound like you're championing desire.

RIDER:
Desires aren't the problem. The problem is that our desires aren't strong enough. At the surface level we feel those de-sires as desperation. We feel scarcity: "There is not enough

to take care of me," or, "I am not enough." We make bad choices when we stop at the surface-level desires. At the core of who we are we want to stop those self-sabotaging choices. If we can have one small moment of awareness we can start to change who we are. One will lead to another and another and this will create a catalytic momentum.

The driver was doubtful.

To him, the smallness of simple situations seemed mundane at best.

DRIVER:
You keep talking about these small moments like you're landing a man on the moon, but sometimes they are just moments.

RIDER:
There are no small moments that don't matter. I had a spine issue that was caused, among other things, by how I got in and out of my car. As silly as it sounds, a doctor pointed out how I cut corners in small moments, thinking I was being efficient, but was actually deforming my muscles in the process.

We can't willfully impose change on our lives and experience long-term benefits. We relax our way into the present moment and notice our desires at the deepest levels. Then let those desires take the place of the distractions.

DRIVER:
What do you mean by relax our way into it? You've probably noticed over the last few hours that I'm not really one for just kicking my feet up and letting the problems solve themselves.

RIDER:

I'm not saying you don't work hard. There is still effort exerted in what you do. Every day you are taking steps to move things forward. You relax with who you are. It's the framework through which we approach the moments and the problems. We aren't moving out of a false energy or false hype. We live from a solid core and bring a relaxed state into what we do. We aren't filled with anxious energy that pushes people away or makes things harder. It will take effort. We struggle and practice and try again.

You can tell when someone else is striving from a place of rage, thirsting for respect from others. They're frantically trying to grab for every scrap they can. And you can tell when someone is synced up, working from congruence. They know who they are and they are focusing their passion and skills on doing that thing. They leave you with a sense of awe because you feel like you're watching something special. There are graspers and there are givers.

You can see those differences in other people and they can see it in you. I want to help people see it in themselves. I want people to live in a space with at least one other person who can see them radiate.

DRIVER:

That's really inspiring. I would love to have that but I don't think I have it in me.

> I stared out the window marked with fingerprints and water stains.

> I could feel the coolness from outside trying to press its way in.

The driver fumbled around with the radio.

The signal was just out of reach.

RIDER:
Let's talk about caterpillars.

He abandoned the lost cause,
his focus drawing in once more.

DRIVER:
What?

RIDER:
There was a group of scientists who studied what happens to a caterpillar when it goes into the cocoon before it becomes a butterfly. They were surprised to find something unusual most people don't know. They discovered that inside the cocoon, the caterpillar turns to goo.

DRIVER:
Goo?

RIDER:
Yeah, like slime. No form, no structure. Just goo inside the cocoon.

DRIVER:
So how does it become a butterfly?

RIDER:
That's the crazy part. The structure for the wings is actually there. They transform from this goo with the structure for wings already present and emerge as a new creature.

The point is, what the caterpillar needs to become a new creation is already within it. The structure for the wings was already there. It just had to be unleashed.

DRIVER:
That's incredible!

RIDER:
It gets even more unbelievable. They took a test group of caterpillars, sprayed a scent around them and zapped them, creating a conditional response to the scent.

DRIVER:
Like Pavlov's dogs.

RIDER:
Yep. They discovered that after the butterflies emerged they still had a negative reaction to the scent.

DRIVER:
Even through the goo transformation?

RIDER:
Amazing, isn't it?

What I'm saying is we can learn how to downshift into the secure desire of who we are. We can relax into a place where the disapproving face that drives us fades away. The strong voice of tradition and the strong voice of others dissipate. We learn to stand in our own identity. We find our own internal guiding north star.

We may have to turn to goo to get there. We may have to go through some painful moments of self-reflection and redefinition but we will find something already within us that aids in our transformation to the next level. We bring the pain from what has happened in the past, but instead of avoiding it we feel it in order to surface the core desires of our identity. From there, we unleash those desires into our mission and community.

> He turned towards me,
> an unsure glance in his eyes.

DRIVER:
That's a big dream. You're talking about taking a deep look in the mirror.

RIDER:
Every day is about growing into the person you want to become. It's about learning to use mistakes for propulsion and learning how to recover under pressure rather than try to remove all pressure from your life. We will make mistakes. We will never entirely extricate ourselves from the stresses of life, so we learn to value deep recovery when we are under the gun of the moment. Then, paradoxically, enjoying the process opens up our greatest performance.

> The driver cleared his throat and rolled down his window so that just a sliver of air could slip in.

DRIVER:
Sounds like you're preparing to take a big leap.

RIDER:
I want to take those jumps, but I take a breath before I do. I relax and improve my peripheral vision. I check my surroundings.

DRIVER:
That's a wise move. Some people jump too far, too fast.

RIDER:
For a lot of people, success gives them a false sense of their strengths and how good they think they are. You will become your own worst enemy if you don't take into account the conditions that helped you achieve past success. If you are secure in the present, you can evaluate past decisions without being defensive. You can recognize when you are distorting reality to force a story you want to be true. Or maybe you dig for one fact to justify what you feel insecurely about and cover up other concerns. So many people are chasing a fantasy and counting on an external factor they can't control.

When we become aware at this level then we know the reasons we hijack our decision-making. Then we do hard work that grows us, not out of fear, but out of gratitude.

DRIVER:
Wait. Gratitude? What does that have to do with anything?

RIDER:
It's the attitude that accompanies our ambition. We aren't climbing from an insecure state that is trying to feel whole through what we do or who we are in relationship with. We climb from a state of gratitude: "This is awesome that I get to do this."

When you understand that you have everything you need already within you, it relaxes you in the moment. You can take the next step with what you already have. When you are secure in who you are, you can be truly grateful.

Not a gratitude weighed down by shame and comparison. Not hyping your way past tough moments. A gratitude that is thankful for the present moment because you know you can grow with who you are, where you are and what you have.

> He rolled down his window a bit more and took a deep belly breath.

> A cool breeze poured into the musty old truck. It was one that ruffled memories of a past that seemed far away.

> The driver rested his arm out the window; his fingers spread as nature's breath rushed over his skin.

DRIVER:
I feel a bit of an epiphany coming on. Now I see it's not about comparing myself or my situation to others. It's not about breaking into a party to feel accepted or whole. I'm feeling like I could get to the point where I enjoy life as it unfolds even when it doesn't meet my expectations. I have surely missed a lot of small moments. But that's something I can change. This sounds weird and feels weird to say but even those clouds in the dark sky look pretty right now.

RIDER:
It sounds like you're ready to transform from that goo phase.

> Blinker on. The truck turned. The canoe shop was ahead.

DRIVER:
Maybe I am ready to make some changes, relax and enjoy

life a little more. I'm not exactly sure where that will take me.

RIDER:
It all feels a little vulnerable and shocking right now, deconstructing everything you have built to this point. Find comfort in knowing you have everything you need to take the next step. Keep showing up in every moment as if it will be one of those magical moments. Not an aggrandized moment. A small moment where you pay attention. You wake up. You notice the pain. You let that pain guide you to the truth of who you are regardless of the shame-based lie that pain often creates. Then you relax.

> The truck came to a stop.

DRIVER:
Is this it?

> The end of our travel together.
> The end of a conversation that spanned miles.

RIDER:
Yeah, looks like we made it. The small moments will give you what you need to build a life you love.

> I shut the door to the truck and began walking towards the canoe shop.

> Peering behind me, I saw the driver lift his hand to me. A few steps and I looked back once more.

> The driver who had stopped his car for me was gone.

7 MISTAKES

1
I don't live from a secure core of who I really am.

2
I am unknowingly guided and driven by fear.

3
I am internally distracted.

4
I am blindly focused on the goal and don't enjoy the process to get there.

5
I make myself responsible for the behavior of others.

6
I insecurely try to be accepted by others.

7
I repeat the same self-sabotaging choices.

there's more

Hype wears off.
Pretending is exhausting.
No more leadership fads.
You glow or fade.

This is for leaders, entrepreneurs,
and those ambitious freaks that want to glow.

FigureThatShiftOut.com

Also if you're interested in having Chris speak for your event:
www.chrismcalister.com/work-with-chris/

Made in the USA
Middletown, DE
21 January 2017